GOD'S BLESSINGS
for YOUR BABY

A Prayer and Scripture Journal for the Mother-to-Be

Kara Quinn-Smith

THOMAS NELSON PUBLISHERS
Nashville

GOD'S BLESSINGS *for* YOUR BABY
A Prayer and Scripture Journal for the Mother-to-Be

Dear Expectant Parent(s),

Congratulations! God is truly blessing you! Psalm 127:3, 4 says, "Children *are* a heritage from the LORD, the fruit of the womb *is* a reward. Like arrows in the hand of a warrior, so *are* the children of one's youth." So you definitely have something to rejoice about as you welcome the blessing of becoming a parent.

On March 13, 1995 the Lord blessed us with a beautiful, healthy baby boy. However, when he was conceived we were a little surprised, as we were just newly married. But God had a plan, and we knew it was His timing. We began to pray God's Word over him right away. One of my first prayers was that this child would shine a light into every person's life that he came across. We are truly seeing that come to pass today! In fact, many people have commented on what a happy, peaceful, loving child God has blessed us with, and many have asked if there were specific prayers we prayed while I was pregnant. The answer was a resounding YES!

Proverbs 4:20-22 says, "My son, give attention to my words; incline your ear to my sayings. Do not let them depart from your eyes; keep them in the midst of your heart; for they *are* life to those who find them, and health to all their flesh."

Use this journal to pray God's words of life into your child, and begin that special bonding process as you build him/her up in the Word. Keep track of your own personal prayers and special moments throughout your pregnancy. What a wonderful gift to pass down to your children when they grow up!

Psalm 139:14 says we are "fearfully and wonderfully made," and God revealed in Jeremiah 1:5, "Before I formed you in the womb I knew you; before you were born I sanctified you."

God promises His blessing to those who obey and trust His Word. You are being blessed! So enjoy this time of preparing for God's special miracle in your life.

Suggestions for use:

- Pray out loud and meditate on daily Scriptures and personal prayers over your baby.

- Pray out loud and meditate on "Scriptures for Mom" each week—you'll also find more topical Scriptures in the back for specific needs.

- Pray for your baby's physical development using the growth information as a guide for each part of your baby as it forms.

- Pray for your baby's spiritual development and temperament (peaceful, loving, wise, joyful, prosperous, etc.).

- Use the journal sections for your own thoughts, dreams, special moments, events and prayers.

- Spend some special quiet time ministering to your unborn child by reading out loud, singing songs, listening to music, or laying hands on your baby.

Kara Quinn-Smith

WELCOME THE BLESSING

Love, Health, Protection,
Strength and Peace

Speak God's Word
Over Your Child

You shall love the LORD your God

with all your heart,

with all your soul,

and with all your strength.

And these words

which I command you today

shall be in your heart.

You shall teach them diligently to your children,

and shall talk of them when you sit in your house,

when you walk by the way,

when you lie down,

and when you rise up.

You shall bind them as a sign on your hand,

and they shall be as frontlets between your eyes.

You shall write them on the doorposts

of your house and on your gates.

Deuteronomy 6:5-9

SCRIPTURES *for* MOM

Children are a heritage
from the LORD, the fruit
of the womb is a reward.
Psalm 127:3

SUNDAY
God blessed them, and
God said to them, "Be
fruitful and multiply;
fill the earth and
subdue it...."
Genesis 1:28

MONDAY
My child is a heritage
from the Lord; the fruit
of my womb is a reward
from Him.
Psalm 127:3

TUESDAY
May You hedge my child
behind and before, and
lay Your hand upon him.
Psalm 139:5

PERSONAL PRAYERS, SCRIPTURES *and* THOUGHTS

....
....
....
....
....
....
....
....
....
....
....
....
....
....
....
....
....
....
....

WEDNESDAY

May my child be an heir of God and a joint heir with Christ.

Romans 8:17

THURSDAY

Lord, please make my child complete in every good work to do Your will, working in him what is well pleasing in Your sight, through Jesus Christ.

Hebrews 13:21

FRIDAY

May my child's steps be ordered by You, Lord, and may You delight in his way.

Psalm 37:23

SATURDAY

May You be my child's refuge and strength, a very present help in trouble.

Psalm 46:1

SCRIPTURES *for* MOM

*Like arrows in the hand
of a warrior, so are the
children of one's youth.*
Psalm 127:4

SUNDAY
*May my child love the
Lord God with all his
heart, with all his soul,
and with all his strength.
And may these words
which are commanded be
in his heart.*
Deuteronomy 6:5, 6

MONDAY
*May my child be Your
workmanship, created in
Christ Jesus for good
works, which God prepared
beforehand that he should
walk in them.*
Ephesians 2:10

TUESDAY
*May my child receive the
words that wisdom teaches,
and treasure its commands
within him, so that he may
incline his ear to wisdom,
and apply his heart to
understanding.*
Proverbs 2:1, 2

12

Week 5

PERSONAL PRAYERS, SCRIPTURES *and* THOUGHTS

WEDNESDAY

May my child be sanctified by the Spirit of God for obedience.

1 Peter 1:2

THURSDAY

Lord, open my child's eyes that he may see wondrous things from Your law.

Psalm 119:18

FRIDAY

May my child be more than a conqueror through Christ who loves him.

Romans 8:37

SATURDAY

Teach my child Your way, O Lord, that he may walk in Your truth. Give him singleness of heart that he may fear Your name.

Psalm 86:11

SCRIPTURES
for MOM

*"For this child I prayed,
and the LORD has granted
me my petition which I
asked of Him."*
1 Samuel 1:27

SUNDAY
*May my child be a partaker
of the divine nature of
God, and may he escape
the depravity that is in the
world through lust.*
2 Peter 1:4

MONDAY
*May wisdom enter my
child's heart, and knowledge
be pleasant to his soul.*
Proverbs 2:10

TUESDAY
*May my child be the salt
of the earth and the light
of the world.*
Matthew 5:13, 14

PERSONAL PRAYERS, SCRIPTURES *and* THOUGHTS

....
....
....
....
....
....
....
....
....
....
....
....
....
....
....
....
....
....
....
....
....

WEDNESDAY

May discretion preserve my child and understanding keep him.

Proverbs 2:11

THURSDAY

May my child be strong in the Lord and in the power of His might.

Ephesians 6:10

FRIDAY

May my child walk in the way of goodness and keep to the paths of righteousness.

Proverbs 2:20

SATURDAY

May my child be complete in Him, who is the head of all rule and authority.

Colossians 2:10

SCRIPTURES
for MOM

"Blessed are you among
women, and blessed is the
fruit of your womb!"
Luke 1:42

SUNDAY

May my child not forget
Your law, but let his heart
keep Your commands; for
length of days and long
life and peace they will
add to him.
Proverbs 3:1, 2

MONDAY

May my child be like a tree
planted by the rivers of
water....May he prosper
in whatever he does.
Psalm 1:3

TUESDAY

May my child not let
mercy and truth forsake
him; may he bind them
around his neck and write
them on the tablet of his
heart.
Proverbs 3:3

PERSONAL PRAYERS, SCRIPTURES *and* THOUGHTS

....
....
....
....
....
....
....
....
....
....
....
....
....
....
....
....
....

WEDNESDAY
May my child become a
child of God and be led by
the Spirit of God.
Romans 8:14

THURSDAY
May my child trust in the
Lord with all his heart,
and lean not to his own
understanding.
Proverbs 3:5

FRIDAY
May God supply all my
child's needs according to
His riches in glory by
Christ Jesus.
Philippians 4:19

SATURDAY
May my child acknowledge
You in all his ways, and
You will direct his paths.
Proverbs 3:6

SCRIPTURES for MOM

And Sarah said, "God has made me laugh, and all who hear will laugh with me....Who would have said to Abraham that Sarah would nurse children?"

Genesis 21:6, 7

SUNDAY

May my child be blessed with every spiritual blessing in the heavenly places in Christ.

Ephesians 1:3

MONDAY

Chasten your son while there is hope, and do not set your heart on his destruction.

Proverbs 19:18

TUESDAY

May my child diligently obey the voice of the Lord God, to observe carefully all His commandments.

Deuteronomy 28:1

PERSONAL PRAYERS, SCRIPTURES and THOUGHTS

....
....
....
....
....
....
....
....
....
....
....
....
....
....
....
....
....
....

....
....
....
....
....
....
....
....
....
....
....
....
....
....
....
....
....
....

WEDNESDAY

*May my child not despise
the chastening of the Lord
nor detest His correction.*

Proverbs 3:11

THURSDAY

*May my child heed the
commandments of the Lord.*

Deuteronomy 28:13

FRIDAY

*May my child know that
whom the Lord loves He
corrects, just as a father
corrects the child in whom
he delights.*

Proverbs 3:12

SATURDAY

*May my child be careful to
observe the commandments
of the Lord.*

Deuteronomy 28:13

19

SCRIPTURES *for* MOM

"Before I formed you in the womb I knew you; before you were born I sanctified you; I ordained you a prophet to the nations."
Jeremiah 1:5

SUNDAY
May my child not be wise in his own eyes, but may he fear the Lord and depart from evil.
Proverbs 3:7

MONDAY
May the Lord open to my child His good treasure and bless all the work of his hands. May my child lend to many nations, but not borrow.
Deuteronomy 28:12

TUESDAY
May my child know that the one who mistreats his father and chases away his mother is a child who causes shame and brings reproach.
Proverbs 19:26

PERSONAL PRAYERS, SCRIPTURES *and* THOUGHTS

....
....
....
....
....
....
....
....
....
....
....
....
....
....
....
....
....

WEDNESDAY

I am persuaded that neither death nor life, nor angels nor principalities nor powers, nor things present nor things to come, nor height nor depth, nor any other created thing, shall be able to separate my child from the love of God which is in Christ Jesus our Lord.

Romans 8:38, 39

THURSDAY

Lord, I pray that my child will find wisdom and gain understanding; then he will be happy.

Proverbs 3:13

FRIDAY

May the Lord make my child increase and abound in love to others.

1 Thessalonians 3:12

SATURDAY

Lord, help me to train up my child in the way he should go, and when he is old, may he not depart from it.

Proverbs 22:6

21

SCRIPTURES *for* MOM

*"Peace I leave with you.
My peace I give to you;
not as the world gives do
I give to you. Let not your
heart be troubled, neither
let it be afraid."*

John 14:27

SUNDAY

*May my child be justified
and glorified through
Christ Jesus.*

Romans 8:30

MONDAY

*Even to my child's old age,
You are God; and even
to his gray hairs You will
carry him! You have
made him.*

Isaiah 46:4

TUESDAY

*May my child be patient
and kind.*

1 Corinthians 13:4

PERSONAL PRAYERS, SCRIPTURES *and* THOUGHTS

WEDNESDAY

*May my child keep sound
wisdom and discretion;
may they be life to his soul
and grace to his neck.*

Proverbs 3:21, 22

THURSDAY

*May my child not envy, be
arrogant, or behave rudely.*

1 Corinthians 13:4, 5

FRIDAY

*I pray my child will not
withhold good from those
to whom it is due, when it
is in the power of his hand
to do so.*

Proverbs 3:27

SATURDAY

*May my child not seek
his own way.*

1 Corinthians 13:5

SCRIPTURES
for MOM

"So you shall serve the LORD your God, and He will bless your bread and your water. And I will take sickness away from the midst of you. No one shall suffer miscarriage or be barren in your land; I will fulfill the number of your days."
Exodus 23:25, 26

SUNDAY
"I have known him, in order that he may command his children and his household after him, that they keep the way of the LORD, to do righteousness and justice."
Genesis 18:19

MONDAY
May my child not be provoked nor keep any account of evil.
1 Corinthians 13:5

PERSONAL PRAYERS,
SCRIPTURES *and* THOUGHTS

....
....
....
....
....
....
....
....
....
....
....
....
....
....
....
....
....
....

TUESDAY

May my child hear the instruction of his father, and not forsake the law of his mother; for they will be a graceful ornament on his head, and chains about his neck.

Proverbs 1:8, 9

WEDNESDAY

May my child not rejoice in iniquity, but rejoice in the truth.

1 Corinthians 13:6

THURSDAY

Lord, help me not to hide Your truths from my child, but tell to the generation to come the praises of the Lord, and His strength and His wonderful works that He has done.

Psalm 78:4

FRIDAY

May my child bear all things and believe all things.

1 Corinthians 13:7

SATURDAY

Out of the mouth of my child may You ordain strength.

Psalm 8:2

SCRIPTURES for MOM

You will keep him in per-fect peace, whose mind is stayed on You, because he trusts in You.
Isaiah 26:3

SUNDAY
May my child hope all things and endure all things.
1 Corinthians 13:7

MONDAY
Please keep my child as the apple of Your eye; hide him under the shadow of Your wings.
Psalm 17:8

TUESDAY
May my child bear the fruit of the Holy Spirit.
Galatians 5:22

PERSONAL PRAYERS, SCRIPTURES and THOUGHTS

....
....
....
....
....
....
....
....
....
....
....
....
....
....
....
....

WEDNESDAY

May my child not forsake wisdom, for wisdom will preserve him.

Proverbs 4:6

THURSDAY

May my child exhibit love as a result of God's Spirit abiding in him.

Galatians 5:22

FRIDAY

May my child know that wisdom is the principal thing. In all his getting, may he get understanding.

Proverbs 4:7

SATURDAY

May my child have joy through God's Spirit abiding in him.

Galatians 5:22

27

SCRIPTURES *for* MOM

Now faith is the substance of things hoped for, the evidence of things not seen.
Hebrews 11:1

SUNDAY
May my child not walk in the way with sinners; Lord, keep his foot from their path.
Proverbs 1:15

MONDAY
May my child have peace through the Spirit of God abiding in him.
Galatians 5:22

TUESDAY
Lord, may my child love the habitation of Your house, and the place where Your glory dwells.
Psalm 26:8

PERSONAL PRAYERS, SCRIPTURES *and* THOUGHTS

....

....

....

....

....

....

....

....

....

....

....

....

....

....

....

....

....

....

WEDNESDAY

May my child exhibit longsuffering through the power of God's Spirit abiding in him.

Galatians 5:22

THURSDAY

May my child lie down and not be afraid; may he lie down and have sweet sleep.

Proverbs 3:24

FRIDAY

May my child exhibit kindness through the power of God's Spirit abiding in him.

Galatians 5:22

SATURDAY

May my child not be afraid of sudden terror, nor of trouble from the wicked when it comes; may the Lord be his confidence.

Proverbs 3:25, 26

Scriptures for MOM

May the God of hope fill
you with all joy and peace
in believing, that you may
abound in hope by the
power of the Holy Spirit.
Romans 15:13

SUNDAY
May my child have good-
ness through the Spirit of
God abiding in him.
Galatians 5:22

MONDAY
May my child hear and
receive wisdom, and the
years of his life will be
many.
Proverbs 4:10

TUESDAY
May my child exhibit
gentleness through the
power of God's Spirit
abiding in him.
Galatians 5:23

Personal Prayers, Scriptures and Thoughts

....
....
....
....
....
....
....
....
....
....
....
....
....
....
....
....
....
....

WEDNESDAY

May my child walk and his steps not be hindered, and when he runs, may he not stumble.

Proverbs 4:12

THURSDAY

May my child exhibit self-control by the power of God's Spirit abiding in him.

Galatians 5:23

FRIDAY

May my child not enter the path of the wicked, and may he not walk in the way of evil.

Proverbs 4:14

SATURDAY

May my child obey his parents in the Lord, for this is right.

Ephesians 6:1

31

SCRIPTURES
for MOM

He forgives all your
iniquities, and heals all
your diseases.
Psalm 103:3

SUNDAY
May my child keep his
heart with all diligence,
for out of it spring the
issues of life.
Proverbs 4:23

MONDAY
May my child honor his
father and mother, which is
the first commandment
with promise: that it may
be well with him and he
may live long on the earth.
Ephesians 6:2, 3

TUESDAY
May You direct my
child's work in truth,
and make with him
an everlasting covenant.
Isaiah 61:8

PERSONAL PRAYERS,
SCRIPTURES *and* THOUGHTS

....
....
....
....
....
....
....
....
....
....
....
....
....
....
....
....
....
....

WEDNESDAY
May my child put on the whole armor of God, that he may be able to stand against the wiles of the devil.
Ephesians 6:11

THURSDAY
May my child be merciful and lend; may his descendants be blessed.
Psalm 37:26

FRIDAY
May my child hear the instruction of his father, and give attention to know understanding.
Proverbs 4:1

SATURDAY
May my child be clothed with the belt of truth.
Ephesians 6:14

SCRIPTURES *for* MOM

The LORD will give
strength to His people;
the LORD will bless His
people with peace.
Psalm 29:11

SUNDAY

*May my child put on the
breastplate of righteousness.*
Ephesians 6:14

MONDAY

*My child, "Let your heart
retain my words; keep my
commands, and live."*
Proverbs 4:4

TUESDAY

*May my child cover his
feet with the preparation
of the gospel of peace.*
Ephesians 6:15

PERSONAL PRAYERS, SCRIPTURES *and* THOUGHTS

....
....
....
....
....
....
....
....
....
....
....
....
....
....
....
....
....
....

WEDNESDAY
May my child get wisdom and understanding; may he not forget nor turn away from wisdom.
Proverbs 4:5

THURSDAY
May my child take up the shield of faith, with which he will be able to quench all the fiery darts of the wicked one.
Ephesians 6:16

FRIDAY
May my child take firm hold of instruction, and not let her go; may he keep her, for she is his life.
Proverbs 4:13

SATURDAY
May my child put on the helmet of salvation.
Ephesians 6:17

SCRIPTURES
for MOM

Be anxious for nothing, but in everything by prayer and supplication, with thanksgiving, let your requests be made known to God.

Philippians 4:6

SUNDAY
May my child's eyes look straight ahead.

Proverbs 4:25

MONDAY
May my child take up the sword of the Spirit, which is the word of God.

Ephesians 6:17

TUESDAY
May my child remember that the ways of man are before the eyes of the Lord, and He ponders all his paths.

Proverbs 5:21

PERSONAL PRAYERS, SCRIPTURES *and* THOUGHTS

....
....
....
....
....
....
....
....
....
....
....
....
....
....
....
....

WEDNESDAY

*May my child not grow
weary in doing good, for in
due season he will reap if
he does not lose heart.*

Galatians 6:9

THURSDAY

*May my child offer to God
thanksgiving, and pay his
vows to the Most High.*

Psalm 50:14

FRIDAY

*May the God of our Lord
Jesus Christ, the Father
of glory, give to my child
the spirit of wisdom and
revelation in the knowledge
of Him.*

Ephesians 1:17

SATURDAY

*May my child keep his
father's command,
and not forsake the law
of his mother.*

Proverbs 6:20

SCRIPTURES
for MOM

I beseech you therefore,
brethren, by the mercies
of God, that you present
your bodies a living
sacrifice, holy, acceptable
to God, which is your
reasonable service.

Romans 12:1

SUNDAY

God has not given my child
a spirit of fear, but of
power and of love and of
a sound mind.

2 Timothy 1:7

MONDAY

Through God may my
child do valiantly.

Psalm 60:12

TUESDAY

May the eyes of my child's
understanding be enlight-
ened, that he may know
what is the hope of
His calling.

Ephesians 1:18

PERSONAL PRAYERS,
SCRIPTURES *and* THOUGHTS

....
....
....
....
....
....
....
....
....
....
....
....
....
....
....
....
....
....

WEDNESDAY

Help me to not provoke my child to wrath, but to bring him up in the training and admonition of the Lord.

Ephesians 6:4

THURSDAY

God is able to make all grace abound toward my child, that he, always having all sufficiency in all things, may have an abundance for every good work.

2 Corinthians 9:8

FRIDAY

May my child give, and it will be given to him; good measure, pressed down, shaken together, and running over will be put into his bosom.

Luke 6:38

SATURDAY

When my child roams, may Your Word lead him; when he sleeps, may Your Word keep him; and when he is awake, may Your Word speak to him.

Proverbs 6:22

SCRIPTURES
for MOM

*Commit your way to the
LORD, trust also in Him,
and He shall bring it
to pass.*
Psalm 37:5

SUNDAY
*A father of the fatherless,
a defender of widows,
is God in His holy
habitation.*
Psalm 68:5

MONDAY
*May You, Lord, be my
child's Shepherd; may he
not lack.*
Psalm 23:1

TUESDAY
*May my child receive
abundance of grace and
the gift of righteousness
and thereby reign in life
through Jesus Christ.*
Romans 5:17

PERSONAL PRAYERS,
SCRIPTURES *and* THOUGHTS

....
....
....
....
....
....
....
....
....
....
....
....
....
....
....
....
....

WEDNESDAY
May my child love without hypocrisy, abhor what is evil, and cling to what is good.
Romans 12:9

THURSDAY
May my child know that the fear of man brings a snare, but whoever trusts in the Lord will be safe.
Proverbs 29:25

FRIDAY
The rod and rebuke give wisdom, but a child left to himself brings shame to his mother.
Proverbs 29:15

SATURDAY
May my child be kindly affectionate to others with brotherly love, in honor giving preference to others.
Romans 12:10

SCRIPTURES *for* MOM

Now this is the confidence
that we have in Him,
that if we ask anything
according to His will,
He hears us.
1 John 5:14

SUNDAY

May my child not lag in
diligence, but be fervent in
spirit, serving the Lord.
Romans 12:11

MONDAY

Correct your son, and he
will give you rest; yes,
he will give delight to
your soul.
Proverbs 29:17

TUESDAY

If it is possible, as much
as depends on my child,
may he live peaceably
with all men.
Romans 12:18

PERSONAL PRAYERS, SCRIPTURES *and* THOUGHTS

....
....
....
....
....
....
....
....
....
....
....
....
....
....
....
....
....

WEDNESDAY

May my child walk by faith, not by sight.

2 Corinthians 5:7

THURSDAY

May my child be patient in tribulation.

Romans 12:12

FRIDAY

Though my child may fall, may he not be utterly cast down; for the Lord upholds him with His hand.

Psalm 37:24

SATURDAY

May my child continue steadfastly in prayer.

Romans 12:12

SCRIPTURES
for MOM

*For He shall give His
angels charge over you, to
keep you in all your ways.*
Psalm 91:11

SUNDAY
*May the Lord God be a
sun and shield for my
child; may the Lord give
grace and glory to him.
May He not withhold any
good thing from my child
as he walks uprightly.*
Psalm 84:11

MONDAY
*May my child distribute
to the needs of the saints;
may he be hospitable.*
Romans 12:13

TUESDAY
*May my child praise You,
O Lord, with all his heart;
may he glorify Your name
forevermore.*
Psalm 86:12

PERSONAL PRAYERS,
SCRIPTURES *and* THOUGHTS

....
....
....
....
....
....
....
....
....
....
....
....
....
....
....
....
....
....
....

WEDNESDAY

May my child find You,
O Lord, to be a God
full of compassion and
gracious, longsuffering
and abundant in mercy
and truth.

Psalm 86:15

THURSDAY

May my child bless those
who persecute him; may he
bless and not curse them.

Romans 12:14

FRIDAY

May my child rejoice with
those who rejoice, and weep
with those who weep.

Romans 12:15

SATURDAY

May Your mercy keep
my child forever, and may
Your covenant stand firm
with him.

Psalm 89:28

SCRIPTURES
for MOM

For the weapons of our
warfare are not carnal but
mighty in God for pulling
down strongholds.
2 Corinthians 10:4

SUNDAY

May my child not be over-
come by evil, but overcome
evil with good.
Romans 12:21

MONDAY

Let Your work appear to
Your servants, and Your
glory to my child.
Psalm 90:16

TUESDAY

May my child be subject
to the governing authorities,
for there is no authority
except from God, and the
authorities that exist are
appointed by God.
Romans 13:1

PERSONAL PRAYERS,
SCRIPTURES *and* THOUGHTS

....
....
....
....
....
....
....
....
....
....
....
....
....
....

May You be my child's
refuge and fortress; being
his God, may he trust
in You.
Psalm 91:2

THURSDAY
May my child love his
neighbor as he loves himself.
Romans 13:9

FRIDAY
May my child owe no
one anything except to love
others, for he who loves
another has fulfilled the law.
Romans 13:8

SATURDAY
God commanded our
fathers that they should
make His commandments
known to their children,
that the generation to
come—my child who
would be born—might
know them, that they might
arise and declare them to
their children.
Psalm 78:5, 6

SCRIPTURES *for* MOM

Whatever is born of God
overcomes the world. And
this is the victory that has
overcome the world—
our faith.

1 John 5:4

SUNDAY

May my child know that
all things are possible to
him who believes.

Mark 9:23

MONDAY

May my child put on the
Lord Jesus Christ, and
make no provision for the
flesh, to fulfill its lusts.

Romans 13:14

TUESDAY

May my child love the
Lord his God with all his
heart, with all his soul,
with all his mind, and
with all his strength.

Mark 12:30

PERSONAL PRAYERS, SCRIPTURES *and* THOUGHTS

....

....

....

....

....

....

....

....

....

....

....

....

....

....

....

....

....

....

WEDNESDAY
May my child be born again, not of corruptible seed but incorruptible, through the word of God which lives and abides forever.
1 Peter 1:23

THURSDAY
May my child honor his father and his mother, that his days may be long upon the land which the Lord his God will give him.
Exodus 20:12

FRIDAY
May my child know the truth, and the truth will make him free.
John 8:32

SATURDAY
May You deliver my child from the snare of the fowler and from the perilous pestilence.
Psalm 91:3

SCRIPTURES *for* MOM

Beloved, I pray that you may prosper in all things and be in health, just as your soul prospers.

3 John 2

SUNDAY

May You cover my child with Your feathers, and under Your wings may he take refuge. May Your truth be his shield and buckler.

Psalm 91:4

MONDAY

May my child not be afraid of the terror by night, nor of the arrow that flies by day.

Psalm 91:5

TUESDAY

Though a thousand may fall at his side and ten thousand at his right hand, may evil not come near my child.

Psalm 91:7

PERSONAL PRAYERS, SCRIPTURES *and* THOUGHTS

....
....
....
....
....
....
....
....
....
....
....
....
....
....
....
....
....

WEDNESDAY

May no evil befall my child, nor any plague come near his dwelling.
Psalm 91:10

THURSDAY

The blessing of the LORD makes one rich, and He adds no sorrow with it.
Proverbs 10:22

FRIDAY

May the Lord always be at my child's right hand, that he may not be shaken.
Acts 2:25

SATURDAY

Lord, give Your angels charge over my child, to keep him in all his ways. May they bear him up in their hands, lest he dashes his foot against a stone.
Psalm 91:11, 12

SCRIPTURES *for* MOM

Let all those rejoice who put their trust in You; let them ever shout for joy, because You defend them; let those also who love Your name be joyful in You.
Psalm 5:11

SUNDAY
The mercy of the LORD is from everlasting to everlasting on those who fear Him, and His righteousness to children's children.
Psalm 103:17

MONDAY
May my child fear the Lord and delight greatly in His commandments. May his descendants be mighty on earth.
Psalm 112:1, 2

TUESDAY
May the Lord give increase more and more to me and my child.
Psalm 115:14

PERSONAL PRAYERS, SCRIPTURES *and* THOUGHTS

....
....
....
....
....
....
....
....
....
....
....
....
....
....
....
....
....

WEDNESDAY
May the Lord preserve my child from this time forth, and even forevermore.
Psalm 121:8

THURSDAY
May the Lord not allow my child's foot to slip. You are the One who keeps him; You will not slumber.
Psalm 121:3

FRIDAY
May the Lord be my child's keeper; may the Lord be his shade at his right hand.
Psalm 121:5

SATURDAY
May my child's mouth be filled with laughter, and his tongue with singing.
Psalm 126:2

Scriptures for Mom

But without faith it is impossible to please Him, for he who comes to God must believe that He is, and that He is a rewarder of those who diligently seek Him.

Hebrews 11:6

SUNDAY

May You keep my child's soul and deliver him; let him not be ashamed as he puts his trust in You.

Psalm 25:20

MONDAY

May You, Lord, perfect that which concerns my child; Your mercy, O Lord, endures forever; do not forsake the works of Your hands.

Psalm 138:8

TUESDAY

May Your word be a lamp to my child's feet and a light to his path.

Psalm 119:105

Personal Prayers, Scriptures and Thoughts

....
....
....
....
....
....
....
....
....
....
....
....
....
....
....
....
....

WEDNESDAY
I will praise You, for my child is fearfully and wonderfully made; marvelous are Your works, and that my soul knows very well.
Psalm 139:14

THURSDAY
May You be my child's hiding place and his shield; may he hope in Your word.
Psalm 119:114

FRIDAY
Your eyes saw my child's substance, being yet unformed, and in Your book they all were written, the days fashioned for him, when as yet there were none of them.
Psalm 139:16

SATURDAY
Lord, please give to my child understanding according to Your word.
Psalm 119:169

SCRIPTURES *for* MOM

Above all, taking the shield of faith with which you will be able to quench all the fiery darts of the wicked one.

Ephesians 6:16

SUNDAY

May You strengthen the bars of my gates; may You bless my child within me.

Psalm 147:13

MONDAY

May my child have the mind of Christ.

1 Corinthians 2:16

TUESDAY

May Christ, who has become a curse for us, redeem my child from the curse of the law.

Galatians 3:13

PERSONAL PRAYERS, SCRIPTURES *and* THOUGHTS

....
....
....
....
....
....
....
....
....
....
....
....
....
....
....
....
....
....
....

....

....

....

....

....

....

....

....

....

....

....

....

....

....

....

....

....

WEDNESDAY

"For I know the thoughts that I think toward you," says the LORD, *"thoughts of peace and not of evil, to give you a future and a hope."*
Jeremiah 29:11

THURSDAY

He who is in you is greater than he who is in the world.
1 John 4:4

FRIDAY

May my child be taught by the Lord, and great shall be the peace of my child.
Isaiah 54:13

SATURDAY

Like arrows in the hand of a warrior, so are the children of one's youth.
Psalm 127:4

SCRIPTURES
for MOM

That your faith should not be in the wisdom of men but in the power of God.

1 Corinthians 2:5

SUNDAY

May the Spirit of the Lord rest upon my child, the Spirit of wisdom and understanding, the Spirit of counsel and might, the Spirit of knowledge and of the fear of the Lord.

Isaiah 11:2

MONDAY

May my child's delight be in the fear of the Lord.

Isaiah 11:3

TUESDAY

May my child know that death and life are in the power of the tongue, and those who love it will eat its fruit.

Proverbs 18:21

PERSONAL PRAYERS, SCRIPTURES *and* THOUGHTS

....
....
....
....
....
....
....
....
....
....
....
....
....
....
....
....
....
....
....

WEDNESDAY

May You pour Your Spirit on my child, Your blessing on my offspring; then they will spring up among the grass like willows by the watercourses.

Isaiah 44:3, 4

THURSDAY

You who made me in the womb made my child. The same One fashioned us in the womb.

Job 31:15

FRIDAY

Lord, please show my child the path of life. In Your presence may he find fullness of joy, and at Your right hand pleasures forevermore.

Psalm 16:11

SATURDAY

May my child not be of this world, just as You are not of this world.

John 17:14

SCRIPTURES
for MOM

Cast your burden on the
LORD, and He shall
sustain you; He shall
never permit the righteous
to be moved.
Psalm 55:22

SUNDAY
May my child say, "I am
the Lord's."
Isaiah 44:5

MONDAY
May my child know that a
wholesome tongue is a tree
of life, but perverseness in
it breaks the spirit.
Proverbs 15:4

TUESDAY
May You hide my child in
the shadow of Your hand.
Isaiah 49:2

PERSONAL PRAYERS,
SCRIPTURES *and* THOUGHTS

....
....
....
....
....
....
....
....
....
....
....
....
....
....
....
....
....
....

WEDNESDAY

May my child press toward the goal for the prize of the upward call of God in Christ Jesus.

Philippians 3:14

THURSDAY

May my child know what the Lord requires of him: to do justly, to love mercy, and to walk humbly with his God.

Micah 6:8

FRIDAY

May You be with my child always, even to the end of the age.

Matthew 28:20

SATURDAY

"I will be a Father to you, and you shall be My sons and daughters," says the LORD *Almighty.*

2 Corinthians 6:18

SCRIPTURES
for MOM

If any of you lacks wisdom, let him ask of God, who gives to all liberally and without reproach, and it will be given to him.

James 1:5

SUNDAY

The Lord says, "In an acceptable time I have heard you, and in the day of salvation I have helped you."

2 Corinthians 6:2

MONDAY

May the grace of the Lord Jesus Christ, and the love of God, and the communion of the Holy Spirit be with my child.

2 Corinthians 13:14

TUESDAY

May my child know that he who sows righteousness will have a sure reward.

Proverbs 11:18

PERSONAL PRAYERS,
SCRIPTURES *and* THOUGHTS

....
....
....
....
....
....
....
....
....
....
....
....
....
....
....
....
....
....
....

WEDNESDAY

May my child be a son of God through faith in Christ Jesus.

Galatians 3:26

THURSDAY

May my child grow and become strong in spirit, filled with wisdom, and may the grace of God be upon him.

Luke 2:40

FRIDAY

May my child be a son of God, and if a son, then an heir of God through Christ.

Galatians 4:7

SATURDAY

May my child know that the generous soul will be made rich, and he who waters will also be watered himself.

Proverbs 11:25

63

SCRIPTURES
for MOM

A man's heart plans his way, but the LORD directs his steps.

Proverbs 16:9

SUNDAY

May my child prosper in all things and be in health, just as his soul prospers.

3 John 2

MONDAY

May my child know that the heart of the prudent acquires knowledge, and the ear of the wise seeks knowledge.

Proverbs 18:15

TUESDAY

May my child know that if he is Christ's, then he is Abraham's seed, and an heir according to the promise.

Galatians 3:29

PERSONAL PRAYERS,
SCRIPTURES *and* THOUGHTS

....
....
....
....
....
....
....
....
....
....
....
....
....
....
....
....
....

WEDNESDAY

May my child be filled with the knowledge of God's will in all wisdom and spiritual understanding.

Colossians 1:9

THURSDAY

He who troubles his own house will inherit the wind, and the fool will be servant to the wise of heart.

Proverbs 11:29

FRIDAY

May my child walk worthy of the Lord, fully pleasing Him, being fruitful in every good work and increasing in the knowledge of God.

Colossians 1:10

SATURDAY

May my child know that the fruit of the righteous is a tree of life, and he who wins souls is wise.

Proverbs 11:30

SCRIPTURES
for MOM

Trust in the LORD with all your heart, and lean not on your own under-standing; in all your ways acknowledge Him, and He shall direct your paths.

Proverbs 3:5, 6

SUNDAY

May my child be strength-ened with all might, according to God's glorious power, for all patience and longsuffering with joy.

Colossians 1:11

MONDAY

May my child sing to the Lord as long as he lives; may he sing praise to God while he has his being.

Psalm 104:33

TUESDAY

May my child know that he can have redemption and the forgiveness of sins through the blood of Christ.

Colossians 1:14

PERSONAL PRAYERS, SCRIPTURES *and* THOUGHTS

WEDNESDAY

May my child obey his parents in all things, for this is well pleasing to the Lord.

Colossians 3:20

THURSDAY

May my child have redemption through the blood of Christ, and the forgiveness of sins, according to the riches of His grace.

Ephesians 1:7

FRIDAY

May my child know that the Lord is faithful; may You establish him and guard him from the evil one.

2 Thessalonians 3:3

SATURDAY

Fathers, do not provoke your children, lest they become discouraged.

Colossians 3:21

SCRIPTURES *for* MOM

"Fear not, for I am with you; be not dismayed, for I am your God. I will strengthen you, yes, I will help you, I will uphold you with My righteous right hand."

Isaiah 41:10

SUNDAY

May my child know that he has been chosen in Christ before the foundation of the world, that he should be holy and without blame before Christ in love.

Ephesians 1:4

MONDAY

Father, please turn the hearts of the fathers to the children, and the hearts of the children to their fathers.

Malachi 4:6

TUESDAY

May my child know that You give knowledge of salvation to Your people by the remission of their sins.

Luke 1:77

PERSONAL PRAYERS, SCRIPTURES *and* THOUGHTS

....
....
....
....
....
....
....
....
....
....
....
....
....
....
....
....
....

WEDNESDAY
*May my child be filled
with the Holy Spirit,
even from my womb.*
Luke 1:15

THURSDAY
*May You grant that my
child might serve You
without fear, in holiness
and righteousness all the
days of his life.*
Luke 1:74, 75

FRIDAY
*May my child's soul
magnify the Lord, and his
spirit rejoice in God our
Savior.*
Luke 1:46, 47

SATURDAY
*May I have joy and glad-
ness, and may many rejoice
at the birth of my child.
May he be great in the
sight of the Lord.*
Luke 1:14, 15

SCRIPTURES
for MOM

*Draw near to God and
He will draw near to you.*
James 4:8

SUNDAY
*May You grant my child,
according to the riches of
Your glory, to be strength-
ened with might through
Your Spirit in the inner
man.*
Ephesians 3:16

MONDAY
*May Christ dwell in my
child's heart through faith.*
Ephesians 3:17

TUESDAY
*May my child be rooted
and grounded in love.*
Ephesians 3:17

PERSONAL PRAYERS, SCRIPTURES and THOUGHTS

....
....
....
....
....
....
....
....
....
....
....
....
....
....
....
....
....
....
....
....

WEDNESDAY

May my child be able to comprehend with all the saints what is the width and length and depth and height—to know the love of Christ which passes knowledge.

Ephesians 3:18, 19

THURSDAY

May my child be filled with all the fullness of God.

Ephesians 3:19

FRIDAY

May my child know that the hand of the diligent will rule, but the lazy man will be put to forced labor.

Proverbs 12:24

SATURDAY

May my child know that God is able to do exceedingly abundantly above all that he could ever ask or think, according to the power that works in him.

Ephesians 3:20

SCRIPTURES *for* MOM

I will both lie down in peace, and sleep; for You alone, O LORD, make me dwell in safety.

Psalm 4:8

SUNDAY

I have no greater joy than to hear that my child walks in the truth.

3 John 4

MONDAY

Now to Him who is able to keep my child from stumbling, and to present him faultless before the presence of His glory with exceeding joy, to God our Savior, who alone is wise, be glory and majesty.

Jude 24, 25

TUESDAY

May my child keep himself from idols.

1 John 5:21

PERSONAL PRAYERS, SCRIPTURES *and* THOUGHTS

....
....
....
....
....
....
....
....
....
....
....
....
....
....
....
....
....
....

WEDNESDAY

May grace and peace be multiplied to my child in the knowledge of God and of Jesus our Lord.

2 Peter 1:2

THURSDAY

May my child be a wise child who heeds his father's instruction, for a scoffer does not listen to rebuke.

Proverbs 13:1

FRIDAY

Behold, what manner of love the Father has bestowed on us, that we should be called children of God!

1 John 3:1

SATURDAY

May my child be a witness to the people, a leader and commander for the people.

Isaiah 55:4

SCRIPTURES
for MOM

Come to Me, all you who labor and are heavy laden, and I will give you rest.
Matthew 11:28

SUNDAY
May Jesus' divine power give to my child all things that pertain to life and godliness, through the knowledge of Him who called us by glory and virtue.
2 Peter 1:3

MONDAY
May my child serve the Lord with gladness and come before His presence with singing.
Psalm 100:2

TUESDAY
May my child humble himself under the mighty hand of God, that He may exalt him in due time.
1 Peter 5:6

PERSONAL PRAYERS,
SCRIPTURES *and* THOUGHTS

....

....

....

....

....

....

....

....

....

....

....

....

....

....

....

....

....

WEDNESDAY
May my child cast all his care upon You, for You care for him.
1 Peter 5:7

THURSDAY
May my child be strong and of good courage; may he not be afraid nor dismayed, for You are with him wherever he goes.
Joshua 1:9

FRIDAY
May my child be filled with the Spirit of God, in wisdom, in understanding, in knowledge, and in all manner of workmanship.
Exodus 31:3

SATURDAY
May my child believe on the Lord Jesus Christ, and he will saved.
Acts 16:31

SCRIPTURES *for* MOM

For God has not given
us a spirit of fear, but
of power and of love
and of a sound mind.

2 Timothy 1:7

SUNDAY

As my child has opportu-
nity, let him do good to all,
especially to those who are
of the household of faith.

Galatians 6:10

MONDAY

May my child know that
he who walks with wise
men will be wise, but the
companion of fools will
be destroyed.

Proverbs 13:20

TUESDAY

May my child know the
riches of the glory of
Christ's inheritance in
the saints, and what is
the exceeding greatness of
His power toward those
who believe.

Ephesians 1:18, 19

PERSONAL PRAYERS, SCRIPTURES *and* THOUGHTS

WEDNESDAY

He who spares his rod hates his son, but he who loves him disciplines him promptly.

Proverbs 13:24

THURSDAY

May goodness and mercy follow my child all the days of his life.

Psalm 23:6

FRIDAY

Though my child may walk through the valley of the shadow of death, may he fear no evil, for You will be with him; may Your rod and staff comfort him.

Psalm 23:4

SATURDAY

Show my child Your ways, O Lord; teach him Your paths. Lead my child in Your truth and teach him, for You are the God of his salvation.

Psalm 25:4, 5

SCRIPTURES *for* MOM

Do not be afraid of sudden terror, nor of trouble from the wicked when it comes; for the LORD will be your confidence.
Proverbs 3:25, 26

SUNDAY
May my child know that it is better to get wisdom than gold, and to get understanding is to be chosen rather than silver.
Proverbs 16:16

MONDAY
May my child be of good courage, and You will strengthen his heart, as he puts his hope in the Lord.
Psalm 31:24

TUESDAY
Lord, instruct my child and teach him in the way he should go; guide him with Your eye.
Psalm 32:8

PERSONAL PRAYERS, SCRIPTURES *and* THOUGHTS

....
....
....
....
....
....
....
....
....
....
....
....
....
....
....
....
....
....

WEDNESDAY

May Your presence go with my child, and may You give him rest.
Exodus 33:14

THURSDAY

May my child know that it is more blessed to give than to receive.
Acts 20:35

FRIDAY

Whatever my child wants others to do to him, may he also do to them, for this is the Law and the Prophets.
Matthew 7:12

SATURDAY

May my child not judge, and he shall not be judged; may he not condemn, and he shall not be condemned; may he forgive, and he shall be forgiven.
Luke 6:37

SCRIPTURES
for MOM

He gives power to the
weak, and to those who
have no might He
increases strength.
Isaiah 40:29

SUNDAY
May the Lord preserve
my child from all evil;
may He preserve his soul.
Psalm 121:7

MONDAY
May my child be poor in
spirit, for then the kingdom
of heaven will be his.
Matthew 5:3

TUESDAY
May my child not set his
mind on high things, but
associate with the humble.
May he not be wise in
his own opinion.
Romans 12:16

PERSONAL PRAYERS,
SCRIPTURES *and* THOUGHTS

....
....
....
....
....
....
....
....
....
....
....
....
....
....
....
....
....
....
....

WEDNESDAY

A wise son makes a father glad, but a foolish man despises his mother.

Proverbs 15:20

THURSDAY

May my child be pure in heart, for then he shall see God.

Matthew 5:8

FRIDAY

May my child be a peace-maker, for then he shall be called a son of God.

Matthew 5:9

SATURDAY

May my child be meek, for then he shall inherit the earth.

Matthew 5:5

SCRIPTURES
for MOM

Be strong in the Lord and
in the power of His might.
Ephesians 6:10

SUNDAY
May my child hunger and
thirst for righteousness,
for then he shall be filled.
Matthew 5:6

MONDAY
The light of the eyes rejoices
the heart, and a good report
makes the bones healthy.
Proverbs 15:30

TUESDAY
Through wisdom a house
is built, and by under-
standing it is established;
by knowledge the rooms
are filled with all precious
and pleasant riches.
Proverbs 24:3, 4

PERSONAL PRAYERS,
SCRIPTURES *and* THOUGHTS

....
....
....
....
....
....
....
....
....
....
....
....
....
....
....
....
....
....

WEDNESDAY

The preparations of the heart belong to man, but the answer of the tongue is from the LORD.

Proverbs 16:1

THURSDAY

The father of the righteous will greatly rejoice, and he who begets a wise child will delight in him.

Proverbs 23:24

FRIDAY

May my child commit his works to the Lord, and his thoughts will be established.

Proverbs 16:3

SATURDAY

May my child not let his heart envy sinners, but be zealous for the fear of the Lord all the day.

Proverbs 23:17

SCRIPTURES
for MOM

Abraham did not waver at the promise of God through unbelief, but was strengthened in faith, giving glory to God, and being fully convinced that what He had promised He was also able to perform.

Romans 4:20, 21

SUNDAY

May my child know that the name of the Lord is a strong tower; the righteous run to it and are safe.

Proverbs 18:10

MONDAY

May my child not over-work to be rich, for riches certainly make themselves wings; they fly away like an eagle toward heaven.

Proverbs 23:4, 5

TUESDAY

May my child know by humility and the fear of the Lord come riches and honor and life.

Proverbs 22:4

PERSONAL PRAYERS,
SCRIPTURES *and* THOUGHTS

....
....
....
....
....
....
....
....
....
....
....
....
....
....
....
....
....
....

WEDNESDAY
*May my child repay no
one evil for evil. May he
have regard for good things
in the sight of all men.*
Romans 12:17

THURSDAY
*A foolish son is the ruin
of his father, and the
contentions of a wife are
a continual dripping.*
Proverbs 19:13

FRIDAY
*Foolishness is bound up in
the heart of a child; the rod
of correction will drive it
far from him.*
Proverbs 22:15

SATURDAY
*Houses and riches are
an inheritance from fathers,
but a prudent wife is
from the LORD.*
Proverbs 19:14

SCRIPTURES
for MOM

But those who wait on
the LORD shall renew their
strength; they shall mount
up with wings like eagles,
they shall run and not be
weary, they shall walk
and not faint.
Isaiah 40:31

SUNDAY
Whoever loves wisdom
makes his father rejoice.
Proverbs 29:3

MONDAY
Even a child is known by
his deeds, whether what he
does is pure and right.
Proverbs 20:11

TUESDAY
She will be saved in childbearing if she continues in
faith, love, and holiness,
with self-control.
1 Timothy 2:15

PERSONAL PRAYERS,
SCRIPTURES *and* THOUGHTS

....
....
....
....
....
....
....
....
....
....
....
....
....
....
....
....
....
....

WEDNESDAY

The righteous man walks in his integrity; his children are blessed after him.

Proverbs 20:7

THURSDAY

May my child let his light so shine before men, that they may see his good works and glorify his Father in heaven.

Matthew 5:16

FRIDAY

In the day of my child's trouble, may he call upon You, for You, O Lord, will answer him.

Psalm 86:7

SATURDAY

May my child be merciful, for then he shall obtain mercy.

Matthew 5:7

PERSONAL PRAYERS
SCRIPTURES *and* THOUGHTS

....

....

....

....

....

....

....

....

....

....

....

....

....

....

....

....

....

....

....

Doctor's Visits

Blessed is the Fruit of Your Womb

DOCTOR'S INFORMATION

Doctor's Name: Dr. Miller, Kurt

Address:

Phone:

Associates (if any):

Office hours:

In case of emergencies (when to call, what to do if you can't reach your doctor):

Notes:

DOCTOR'S VISIT

Next appointment time and date: ....

....

Medical notes: ....

....

....

....

....

....

....

....

....

MY BABY'S DEVELOPMENT
Four Weeks Since Conception
Gestational Age—Six Weeks

Your baby at this time is less than $1/4$ of an inch in length.
Growth is rapid during the fourth week.
* The brain is growing and developing distinct regions.
* Eyes and ears are beginning to form.
* Mouth is forming.
* Neck and lower jaw will begin to take shape.
* Heart is already starting to pump blood; backbone, ribs
and muscles of back and sides will form.

DOCTOR'S VISIT

Next appointment time and date: ....

....

Medical notes: ....

....

....

....

....

....

....

....

....

MY BABY'S DEVELOPMENT
Five Weeks Since Conception
Gestational Age—Seven Weeks

Your baby at this time is about 1/3 of an inch in length.

* Brain continues to develop in complexity.
* Cavities and passages for circulation of spinal fluid
  have formed.
* Lenses of eyes are forming; middle ears continue to develop.
* Arms, legs, hands, and feet are taking shape.

DOCTOR'S VISIT

Next appointment time and date: ....

....

Medical notes: ....

....

....

....

....

....

....

....

....

MY BABY'S DEVELOPMENT
Six Weeks Since Conception
Gestational Age—Eight Weeks

Your baby at this time is just over $1/2$ of an inch in length.
- Eyelids are beginning to form.
- Pituitary gland is forming.
- Arms are growing; wrists and elbows are evident.
- Ears, hands, feet, and fingers are beginning to take shape.
- Heart is pumping about 150 beats per minute, about twice the adult rate.

DOCTOR'S VISIT

March 1, 2001

Next appointment time and date: March 29, 2001

Medical notes: I had an ultrasound today everything looks great - nothing abnormal noted.
Due date is officially October 12, 2001.
Seeing my baby made it all so real - what a miracle!

MY BABY'S DEVELOPMENT

Seven Weeks Since Conception
Gestational Age—Nine Weeks

Your baby at this time is 1 inch in length.
- The embryonic tail is disappearing.
- The face is rounded.
- Fingers and toes are forming.
- The pancreas, bile ducts and gallbladder have formed.
- The male and female reproductive organs are starting to develop.

DOCTOR'S VISIT

Next appointment time and date: ....

....

Medical notes: ....

....

....

....

....

....

....

....

....

MY BABY'S DEVELOPMENT

Eight Weeks Since Conception
Gestational Age—Ten Weeks

Your baby at this time is about $1\frac{1}{4}$ inches from head to rump.

- All major body organs have been formed.
- Bones of the skeleton are forming.
- Fingers have formed.
- Eyelids have grown.
- Outer ears are forming.

DOCTOR'S VISIT

March 29, 2001

Next appointment time and date: ....

....

Medical notes: ....

....

....

....

....

....

....

....

....

MY BABY'S DEVELOPMENT

Nine to Twelve Weeks Since Conception
Gestational Age—Eleven to Fourteen Weeks

Your baby is now called a fetus and is about 3 inches in length.
Weighs approximately $1\frac{1}{2}$ ounces.
- All organ systems are in place.
- Brain, nerves and muscles are starting to function.
- The palate is completely formed.
- Genitals are beginning to have characteristics.
- Baby jerks, flexes and kicks.

DOCTOR'S VISIT

Next appointment time and date: ....

....

Medical notes: ....

....

....

....

....

....

....

....

MY BABY'S DEVELOPMENT
Thirteen to Sixteen Weeks Since Conception
Gestational Age—Fifteen to Eighteen Weeks

Your baby at this time is about $5^1/2$ inches in length.
Weighs approximately 7 ounces.
* Eyes and ears have baby-like appearance.
* Eyebrows and scalp hair start to appear.
* Baby has frequent episodes of hiccups.
* Teeth are beginning to form underneath the gums.

DOCTOR'S VISIT

Next appointment time and date: ....

....

Medical notes: ....

....

....

....

....

....

....

....

....

....

MY BABY'S DEVELOPMENT

Seventeen to Twenty Weeks Since Conception
Gestational Age—Nineteen to Twenty-Two Weeks

Your baby at this time is about $7^1/_2$ inches in length from head to rump.
Weighs approximately 1 pound.
* Fine down-like hair covers the skin.
* The kidneys are beginning to make urine.
* Female's vagina, uterus and fallopian tubes have formed.
* Baby can hear and react to sounds.
* Baby's movements may be felt by mother.

DOCTOR'S VISIT

Next appointment time and date: ....

....

Medical notes: ....

....

....

....

....

....

....

....

....

MY BABY'S DEVELOPMENT

Twenty-one to Twenty-four Weeks Since Conception
Gestational Age—Twenty-three to Twenty-six Weeks

Your baby at this time is about 9 inches long.

Weighs approximately 2 pounds.

- Baby's body begins to fill out; weight gain is rapid.
- Bones begin to harden through deposits of calcium.
- Air sacs in the lungs begin to develop.
- Nostrils begin to open.

DOCTOR'S VISIT

Next appointment time and date: ....
....

Medical notes: ....
....
....
....
....
....
....
....
....
....

MY BABY'S DEVELOPMENT

Twenty-five to Twenty-eight Weeks Since Conception
Gestational Age—Twenty-seven to Thirty Weeks

Your baby at this time is about 11 inches long.
Weighs approximately 3 pounds.
* Eyelids begin to open; retinas begin to form.
* Hair on head is growing longer.
* Taste buds are developed.
* Brain is enlarging; sections are beginning to form.
* Baby recognizes mother's voice.

DOCTOR'S VISIT

Next appointment time and date: ....

....

Medical notes: ....

....

....

....

....

....

....

....

....

MY BABY'S DEVELOPMENT

Twenty-nine to Thirty-two Weeks Since Conception
Gestational Age—Thirty-one to Thirty-four Weeks

Your baby at this time is about 17 inches long.

Weighs approximately $4^1/2$ pounds.

- Brain and nerves are maturing.
- Five senses are functional.
- Fingernails have grown past fingertips.
- Male's testicles descend from abdomen to scrotum.
- Baby acquires immunities to infections.

DOCTOR'S VISIT

Next appointment time and date: ....

....

Medical notes: ....

....

....

....

....

....

....

....

....

....

MY BABY'S DEVELOPMENT

Thirty-three to Thirty-eight Weeks Since Conception
Gestational Age—Thirty-five to Forty Weeks

Your baby at this time is about 20 inches long.

Weighs approximately 7$\frac{1}{2}$ pounds.

- Arms and legs are beginning to fatten.
- Creases in neck and wrists are forming from fat.
- Baby turns toward light.
- Baby's grasp is firm.
- Baby gains about an ounce per day.
- Baby assumes position for delivery.

DOCTOR'S VISIT

Next appointment time and date: ....

....

Medical notes: ....

....

....

....

....

....

....

....

....

....

....

....

....

....

....

....

DOCTOR'S VISIT

Next appointment time and date: ....

....

Medical notes: ....

....

....

....

....

....

....

....

....

....

....

....

....

....

....

....

Doctor's Visit

Next appointment time and date: ....

....

Medical notes: ....

....

....

....

....

....

....

....

....

....

....

....

....

....

....

DOCTOR'S VISIT

Next appointment time and date: ....
....

Medical notes: ....
....
....
....
....
....
....
....
....
....
....
....
....
....
....
....

DOCTOR'S VISIT

Next appointment time and date: ....

....

Medical notes: ....

....

....

....

....

....

....

....

....

....

....

....

....

....

....

....

BELIEVING FOR THE BLESSING

*Expectation, Hope,
Encouragement
and Thanksgiving*

Kellee is our second child. I became pregnant with her when I was 39 years old. Because of my age and a previous miscarriage, I was considered a high-risk mother by the doctors, so extra monitoring was given to me.

I was blessed to have a born-again believer as my primary obstetrician. However, because I was in an HMO, other physicians could see me on a given visit.

Another physician examined me and reviewed my most recent ultrasound. She became concerned and wrote on my chart "possible growth retardation." The test "appeared" to show that Kellee was not growing normally. My husband, Keith, and I immediately began to pray and refused to receive the negative report. We began to diligently pray God's Word over Kellee every day and night.

During the last month of my pregnancy, I was required to go to the hospital for an ultrasound and stress test twice a week. Nothing in the natural seemed to change, but my husband and I kept our belief in God's Word.

One night while I was asleep, I had a vision of Kellee. I saw her peering out at me with big round eyes through the slats of her crib. God had confirmed with that dream that all was indeed well.

Kellee was born Sunday, October 29, 1995 weighing 7 pounds, 9 ounces—a very healthy and normal size! One of the first things my doctor said was, "That hospital needs to get its ultrasound machine fixed." Praise the Lord!

CHRISTINE
A Faithful Delivery

When I look at my infant daughter today, the overwhelming thought I have is that our God is an awesome God, so faithful to His Word.

Christine Irene is an answer to a long-standing prayer and a stand of faith that began more than 23 years ago when my husband and I decided to believe God for the desire of our hearts—a child born out of our marriage and love for one another.

As a 19-year-old young lady, newly wed, I had developed problems with my tubes; eventually they became entangled and ruined. My husband and I desperately wanted to have a baby, so I began seeing a doctor who said it would be almost impossible for me to conceive. I began seeing another doctor who tried to work with us in getting pregnant, but she was unsuccessful. It was then that my husband and I decided to take a stand and just believe God for our baby girl.

As my husband and I learned how to walk by faith, we began putting our faith into practice by standing and believing God for everything we needed and desired. But believing for our daughter was our biggest challenge. Despite the dim view of the doctors, we never, ever gave up. And even though we eventually adopted a little five-year-old boy, who is now 16 years old, we continued to believe for our baby girl.

It finally happened. One day I began to experience strange feelings in my body. I immediately thought something was wrong with me because I had never been pregnant before. The enemy immediately came with negative thoughts of sickness and disease, but I began to think to myself that I could be pregnant. A home pregnancy test confirmed my thoughts! I immediately called my doctor who told me not to rely on the home test, because they were not always accurate. But inside, I knew I was pregnant.

Christine Irene was born when I was 43 years old. What a blessing! My husband and I are happy beyond words! We are confident now that after this miracle, we can stand on God's Word for anything.

Reprint with permission, "Ever Increasing Faith Messenger," June/July 1996, Crenshaw Christian Center, Los Angeles, CA

DAVID
The Worshiper

When we were first married, my husband and I decided that we wanted to have two or three children, depending on God's direction. After having two girls, we seriously considered adopting a biracial child through an inner-city ministry. When that did not work out, we believed that perhaps God's plan for us was to have only two children. But He had a surprise for us! Even though we were using birth control, David was conceived. So we knew in our hearts that God had planned him all along. We believed that God's hand was in David's birth and would also be on his life.

After each of our children was born, we began to pray for them daily. We asked God to give us wisdom and insight into what He wanted to bring out of each one. Each evening we would play worship music as the children went to sleep, and then we would pray over them as they slept.

David was the child that sent me to my knees the most. He began school at age four, which was too early for him. I watched problems with self-esteem develop as he struggled in each grade. I was overcome at times with guilt and found myself in agonizing prayer asking God to help David discover the abilities God had given him, and to be able to someday be proud of who God had created him to be.

115

Prayers began to be answered! He was athletically built and discovered a love for sports, which became an outlet for him as he went through grade school. Then, in the 5th grade, he discovered an interest in music and soon began trumpet lessons. We saw the musical ability God had given him, and prayed for that to come forth. David played his trumpet in the jazz band at school, and even took piano lessons for one year in high school. But, eventually, as music wasn't the "macho" thing to be involved with, it took a back seat to athletics once again. It was exciting to see his physical and athletic abilities develop, but God kept showing me that David was full of music, and God wanted to use David for His glory in that area.

David accepted the Lord as his Savior when he was in grade school. He was always involved in church youth group activities, but a total commitment to the Lord was missing in his life. There was a heritage of pastors on my husband's side going back three generations. But when anyone suggested to David that he might also be a pastor, he made it clear that that was out of the question. My husband and I kept praying for God to bring forth what He wanted to do in David's life.

When David graduated from high school, we were delighted

that he chose to spend a year with a missionary group, Youth With a Mission. Since attending college was not something he was considering, we believed God would use this time as a blessing to him. Our prayers were for God to unlock and release what He had for David through the influence of this ministry.

God was faithful! While at Youth With a Mission, David taught himself to play the guitar and was eventually asked to lead the worship time for his team. We were surprised at how well he played the guitar, even without formal lessons. God seemed to bless the talent He had given David. Not only was he playing an instrument in praise to the Lord; he was also singing! His heart was coming through his worship—his heart was after God. We were in awe at what God was doing in his life. Our prayers were being answered even beyond our expectations. Indeed, God was doing exceedingly abundantly more than we could have ever asked.

When David's Youth With a Mission training was finished, he accepted an invitation to be on staff as a worship leader for a men's ministry in Montana. After a two-year commitment with that ministry, David felt led by the Lord to come back home to help with a newly formed church. David believed that God would use him in the area of worship—and indeed God did! Within six months, David was leading the worship band. Over the past two years, we have watched God's working in David's life. He is now serving as part-time pastor, leading the church in worship, and writing worship songs of his own. He is even considering pursuing a degree in music.

David is just as amazed as we are at how God has touched and used his life. Recently, David said to me, "Mom, you always kept telling me God had put a lot of music in me." Now David believes it. He has truly become a worshiper of God from his innermost being.

When we got married, my husband, Chris, and I agreed that we would wait three years before starting our family. We wanted to have time to spend with one another and allow the Lord to solidify our marriage before children came along.

I remember when our third anniversary finally came and we stopped using birth control. I was so excited to actually be trying to have a baby, that I didn't think much of it when, at the end of the first month, I wasn't pregnant. But one month stretched into three, then three into six, then nine. After about a year and a half, I began to fear that I would never be able to conceive.

You see, when I first got married, I remember watching other women around me—friends, coworkers, family members—suffer with infertility. I also remember reading articles and seeing news shows chronicling the growing problem of infertility. For a moment, I'd secretly wondered if I would suffer their fate, but would quickly put that thought in the back of my mind.

But now the fear had returned and hounded me as, month after month, we waited to hear some good news. Some nights I'd pray, "Lord, were we being arrogant or selfish for wanting to wait to have a family? Did we miss our opportunity?"

I began to study God's Word, and the Holy Spirit showed me that children were a gift from the Lord. That excited me at first, because I knew that God's gifts were freely given. But my mind kept telling me that we had missed our opportunity to receive His gift. So I delved deeper into the Word. This time the Holy Spirit reminded me that God's mercies are new every morning. I grabbed hold of that truth and continued my search through the Scriptures.

When I came to the stories of Sarah and Hannah and how the Lord blessed them both to conceive, I was relieved. I thought surely if God would bless them, He'd bless me too. I prayed Hannah's prayer and waited in expectancy. Nothing happened.

Then one day the Holy Spirit showed me that the fear of infertility—that I had neatly tucked away in the back of my mind early in our marriage—had taken root. I knew there was only one way to rid myself of it: the Word of God.

I began to pray and believe that my womb would be a lively place, and that I would be a fruitful vine. I prayed and believed God's Word when I woke up in the morning, all during the day, and before I went to bed at night. I made a special effort to pray when, at the end of the month, I was still not pregnant.

I prayed until God's promises became so real to me, that any day I expected to hear the confirmation in the natural of what I knew had already taken place in the spirit.

That day finally came, and today I am happy to testify that God's Word is true! I am now the proud mother of not one, but two beautiful girls, and my husband and I have already begun to believe God for our third.

I now know that, whatever I can believe God for, He will deliver, because with Him all things are possible.

VICTORIA
A Joy to Love

*S*econd Corinthians 5:17 says, "Therefore if anyone is in Christ, he is a new creation; old things have passed away; behold, all things have become new." I had to come to this conclusion before I could receive the blessing of becoming a mother. Even though I have always loved children, I vowed that I would never have any myself. This decision stemmed from my childhood. My parents legally separated when I was young, and this left my mother very bitter and verbally abusive.

I believe my mother loved me, but my siblings and I were raised in a very strict household, without much freedom to express ourselves as children should. Most of the time we felt confined and rejected. The fear and hurt I felt had gotten so bad that, at the age of twelve, I tried to commit suicide. Thank God for His mercy and His grace.

Proverbs 18:21 says that death and life are in the power of the tongue, and unfortunately my mother's abusive words caused me to dread the idea of ever having children. I had made that promise to myself in my heart and mind, but God had other plans.

I was born again at the age of fifteen, and at the age of twenty-three, before I was even married, God began to deal with me about my inner vow. But in spite of His prompting, I was reticent. The fear of repeating my childhood experiences on my own children had a firm grip on me. Yet my love for children still surfaced. I would spoil everyone else's children, but I still couldn't bring myself to open my heart to having children of my own.

One night the Spirit of the Lord was on me so much that I could not go to sleep. The Lord again was urging me to face my fear, but this time He became even more specific. He began to talk to me about having a baby girl. I remember saying, "Lord, I didn't ask you for a daughter. I never even thought about having a girl." As He spoke, I felt my heart begin to soften.

Soon I was responding, "Well, even if I did have a baby, I'd figure it would be a boy. What would I name a girl?" The Lord spoke ever so softly to me, "Victoria Joy"—"Victoria" to let me know that I would have the victory over my fears, and "Joy" to describe the feeling I'd have as I watched her respond to the love that He'd teach me to shower on her. I still wasn't entirely convinced though. It took a few more years of gentle urging to convince me to release my fear. But God never gives up.

Meanwhile, a surprising revelation occurred. I had gone to the doctor for a routine physical and was told that I would never be able to have children anyway. Apparently, my fallopian tubes were so small that I was unable to ovulate. The doctor's report didn't upset me, because it only confirmed what was in my heart, and I saw how the vow I'd made caused my body to respond by shutting down my reproductive system. But God never gives up.

Shortly after that God spoke to me through an acquaintance. She said, "Sister, I believe God is getting ready to open your womb and heal your body. Get the baby's room ready!" Suddenly, on that hot July day, my eyes of understanding were opened, and my heart was changed in an instant. I received that word with joy!

My husband and I began to pray the Word of God over my body daily. We especially stood on Psalm 113:9, which says that the Lord "grants the barren woman a home, like a joyful mother of children." I began to window shop for baby clothes and baby furniture, and by the time November came, I was bubbling over with faith. No one could tell me that I wouldn't conceive!

I constantly prayed that God would make me fruitful, and had to laugh at the irony of it all. Not a year earlier God had to keep reminding me of His Word, and now here I was doing the same thing. God is so merciful, and without fail He made good on His Word without delay. For the very next month, December 1993, I conceived, and on September 12, 1994, Victoria Joy entered our lives and changed my heart forever. Praise the Lord!

In late July, 1994, I took a home pregnancy test and it came out positive. Expecting feelings of anxiety and fear, all I could feel was the Lord's presence. I was enveloped in His warmth, love and peace. It was then that I knew everything was going to be all right.

You see, this was my third unplanned pregnancy. Unfortunately the first two pregnancies ended in abortion. But this time was different; this time I had Jesus in my life.

The first time I got pregnant, I had an abortion because I thought I could not provide financially or emotionally for a child, and that I was too young and incapable. I honestly thought it was the best thing for the baby. But all of this was a lie that I bought into and went ahead to take the "easy" way out.

When the procedure was over, I was supposed to feel relieved—but I didn't. In fact, I knew something was terribly wrong, and that I had just made one of the biggest mistakes of my life. I also knew deep down that this would affect me far more than anyone had told me.

I began to feel depressed, anxious, empty, ashamed and totally out of control. It also led to many more wrong decisions, including another abortion. After that, I truly hit rock bottom—overwhelmed with depression, more anxiety, fear and finally thoughts of suicide.

Praise God—at this time He directed my husband-to-be into my life to witness to me God's lovingkindness and forgiveness! Eventually I gave my life over to Jesus. This is where God's truth came in and my healing process began.

Facing my third pregnancy, I began to see the same circumstances that caused me to abort the first one. But God showed my husband and me that He would provide for us and the baby, and He did! Each day, throughout my pregnancy, He showed me how to build up the baby growing inside of me with His Word and His wisdom from Proverbs. He showed me how to pray for the baby's development, both physical and spiritual. My husband and I also prayed that God would provide all of the things we needed for the baby such as baby furniture, strollers, etc. True to His promises, God supplied us with everything we needed—a crib, high chair, clothes, toys, diapers, three strollers, and even more—two weeks before the baby was born! God not only gave us what we needed; He gave us above and beyond what we had asked!

But the most awesome blessing was giving birth to a happy,

healthy, beautiful baby boy, named Zechariah David.

God faithfully showed me His truth about children, and He completely changed my heart during this pregnancy. When I would feel guilty as I watched this baby form, He'd remind me of His forgiveness, that He had washed me and made me whiter than snow! When I would feel anxious about supporting this baby, He'd remind me to cast my cares on Him and that all of our needs would be met. He guided me through His Word and showed me how He sees children: They are a blessing, and He knows them before they are even formed in the womb! God has a plan!

My healing from the abortions continues daily, as I have learned to trust in the Lord and receive the mercy and grace He has so freely given me. Most of my healing took place while participating in a post-abortion Bible study at Chicago Care Crisis Pregnancy Centers. It was there that I truly began to understand my relationship with Jesus and receive His love for me.

God says He gives us blessings and adds no sorrow— Zechariah is truly a blessing!

Praise God!

JANNA
Desire of Our Hearts

Even as a child, I loved babies and younger children. I wanted to be a mother more than anything else. When my husband and I married, my heart's desire was to have children as soon as possible—even though it was beginning to be the "in" thing for women to have careers first before thinking about starting their families. Sooner than we expected, I conceived, and we were elated! Our hopes and dreams were dashed, though, when almost four months into the pregnancy we lost the baby. My faith was strong enough that I didn't question God, but my heart was broken, and I wondered if I would ever have a baby. I remember asking the Lord to take the longing and desire out of my heart if it was not in His plan for us to have children.

God answered that prayer by making the desire in my heart even stronger. About three years later, in His own timing, God blessed us with a precious baby boy. And in just over five years, God entrusted two more baby boys—bundles of joy and delight—into the care of our family. Wow! Three special gifts from God in such a short time—we were so blessed! Everyone thought that surely our quiver was full! But, as long as we could remember, my husband and I had always believed we would have four children, and we prayed to that end.

Sure enough, in less than two years after the birth of our third son, I conceived again. This time, however, we lost the baby. We were heartbroken, but resolved to "try again" as soon as we could. God, in His wisdom and love, chose a path for us that we would never have chosen for ourselves. In 16 months time, I suffered three miscarriages. After the third one, I remember falling across the bed in the outpatient room of the hospital and saying, "God, I can't do this again!" I begged Him to take away the pain and the longing in my heart to have one more baby. Emotional devastation and spiritual doubt set in. Even some of our best friends and fellow believers could not understand our desire for a fourth child. But my obstetrician, who was a mature believer in Christ, encouraged us and prayed with us through those heartrending months.

As we prayed and surrendered ourselves to our sovereign God, we had great peace that He had not forsaken us, that He had not made any mistakes, that He loved us with an everlasting love, and that He knew what was best for our family. We totally gave our dreams and desires to Him and yielded ourselves to His control. I remember the doctor saying, shortly after the third miscarriage, "If God has put the desire in your heart to have another baby, He will give you another baby! I'm not saying that there won't be another miscarriage or maybe even three more miscarriages. But God will either give you the desire of your hearts, or He will take the desire out of your hearts!"

God did just that! Today, Janna Deborah, our fourth gift from God's hand, is a beautiful 10-year-old with a hearty laugh like mom's and a tender heart like dad's!

God is so faithful to His Word! He asks us to be obedient to Him today, and to trust Him for tomorrow—for *His* best for our lives, whatever that may be.

Elizabeth, our precious girl, has finally arrived. Over three years of struggle have come to an end. We have endured the loss of a premature son and two miscarriages during our journey. The grief has been immense, but the knowledge that our God has promised never to leave us nor forsake us has been the comfort—and the hope—we have clung to. We have come to trust in His sovereignty in our lives and know that His timing is perfect.

During those dark days, when my maternal heart was heavy with the longing for a child, I pleaded with the Lord to show me His path for my life. Perhaps He wanted something other than motherhood for me? Oh, how I wanted the skies to part and God's unmistakable voice to plainly make His way known! But that was not His plan for me, for He wanted me, ever in need of "evidence," to learn to trust Him in the absence of signs. He wanted to grow my faith in the desert before he brought me to the Promised Land. Would I believe that all things work for good to those who love God, even if that meant not having a child? The agony and loneliness of it all was almost unbearable. But surely my trust in Him blossomed, as did my husband's. Control had to be given to God.

When I finally became pregnant with Elizabeth, we celebrated hesitantly. Not quite sure if the result of this pregnancy would be a full term baby, we cautiously planned our baby's arrival. Weekly doctor's visits, countless ultrasounds, exhausting treatments to keep our baby alive in my womb were our tasks. Daily we prayed that our hearts would be focused on God and that we would seek Him, the Giver—that we would accept whatever gift He had for us. People all over the country prayed with us in faith and hope that God's will for us would be a child.

When we reached that critical 28th week of pregnancy—when a baby has an excellent chance of survival—we sighed with relief. We continued to pray for the Lord's grace in our lives, and we dedicated our unborn child to His service.

During the 35th week of pregnancy, our daughter burst forth with a hearty wail and robust health. We cried with joy as we held God's precious gift to us in our arms. Praising God for giving us a child, we realized how far we had come! We had been able to minister to others dealing with infertility because of our own struggle. We could better comfort those who had lost children because of our own loss. Indeed, our heavenly Father had used everything—even the heartache—for His glory. And now as we embark on parenthood, we know that He will again bless us as we serve Him. We gaze lovingly at Elizabeth—our miracle baby—and know that God will continue to grow us all in faith as we continue to give our lives to Him.

HANNAH
Devoted to Prayer

It all started in January, 1998. My husband and I had been discussing whether or not it was time for us to begin a family, but I wasn't sure if the time was right. I began to pray about it and ask God to show us His plan. Considering my health problems—including endometriosis—we knew that it would be a real challenge for me to get pregnant.

Within the first couple of weeks of January, I started to consider children's names, always praying for the Lord's will for our family. My desire was to have a girl, and I kept thinking of the name *Hannah*. I remembered this name was in the Old Testament somewhere, but I wasn't familiar with her story.

On January 22, I mentioned to my unsaved family that I'd someday like to have a girl and name her Hannah. At this time, we still weren't sure when we should begin our family. We wanted complete direction from the Lord concerning His timing.

Late that evening, I could not sleep and felt burdened to spend time with the Lord in prayer and the Word. I began thanking and praising God for the thoughts about Hannah and having children. I continued to ask Him to reveal His will for our family and lifted up all my concerns to Him. I humbly expressed my desire to the Lord for a baby girl, and told Him that I wanted to name her Hannah. I opened my Bible and continued with a Bible study I had begun weeks before. That evening my study was on becoming a woman of prayer. The second question in the study directed me to I Samuel I where the story of Hannah is told. I read the passage and was so excited to read about her devotion to the Lord! Not only did I love the name *Hannah*, but I was also thrilled with the kind of woman she was—the same kind of woman I would like our Hannah to become. I remember thinking, "What a great way to witness to unbelievers by telling them the story of our daughter!"

After time in prayer and seeking the Lord's direction, I believed that God was telling us to begin a family right away. I was filled with awe and joy! I believed, by faith, that God was going to bless us with a baby girl. I believe it was God-ordained that the day I discussed baby names with my family was the same day I was led to the Old Testament story of Hannah. Two weeks after that night spent in prayer and study of God's Word, I conceived. It was such a wonderful and blessed surprise when the pregnancy was confirmed! My husband and I rejoiced together in God's goodness!

All through the pregnancy I believed the baby would be our Hannah. Through those nine months, there were times of doubt, but God kept taking me back to the night of January 22. I felt strongly that He had answered my prayer and blessed us with a girl.

The months of pregnancy were an awesome time, because it became a witness and testimony to my unsaved family of God's goodness to us. I shared my story with a lot of people, believing that God would be faithful to give us a girl. On October 11, 1998, He proved His faithfulness—Hannah Elise was born. Every day I pray that our Hannah will follow the example of her namesake and become a woman dedicated to God in prayer.

Preparing for the Blessing

Enlarge Your House;
Build an Addition;
Spread out Your Home!

BABY SHOWER GUESTS AND GIFTS

....

....

....

....

....

....

....

....

....

....

....

....

....

....

....

....

....

....

....

....

Every good gift and every perfect gift is from above, and comes down from the Father of lights, with whom there is no variation or shadow of turning.

James 1:17

And when they had come into the house, they saw the young Child with Mary His mother....And when they had opened their treasures, they presented gifts to Him: gold, frankincense, and myrrh.

Matthew 2:11

BABY SHOWER GUESTS AND GIFTS

....

....

....

....

....

....

....

....

....

....

....

....

....

....

....

....

....

....

....

....

Blessed Labor & Delivery

Faith, Comfort,
Lively and Quickly Delivered

....

....

....

....

....

....

....

....

....

....

....

....

....

....

....

She will be saved in childbearing if they continue
in faith, love, and holiness, with self-control.
1 Timothy 2:15

Baby's full name: ....

....

Date and time of arrival: ....

....

Name of Hospital: ....

....

Address, City and State: ....

....

....

Delivered by: ....

Nurse: ....

Pediatrician: ....

Weight: ....

Height: ....

Hair: ....

Eyes: ....

Birthmarks: ....

And Sarah said, "God has made me laugh, and all who hear
will laugh with me." She also said, "Who would have said to
Abraham that Sarah would nurse children?"

Genesis 21:6, 7

144

OUR FIRST THOUGHTS
AND REACTIONS...

....

....

....

....

....

....

And all those who heard them kept them in their hearts, saying,
"What kind of child will this be?" And the hand of the Lord was with him.
Luke 1:66

BABY'S FIRST VISITORS

....

....

....

....

....

....

....

When her neighbors and relatives heard how the Lord had shown
great mercy to her, they rejoiced with her.
Luke 1:58

BABY'S DEDICATION

Date: ....

....

Pastor/Reverend: ....

....

Church: ....

....

Godparents: ....

....

....

....

....

"For this child I prayed, and the LORD has granted me my
petition which I asked of Him. Therefore I also have lent him
to the LORD; as long as he lives he shall be lent to the LORD."
1 Samuel 1:27, 28

TOPICAL SCRIPTURES

Prayers, Thoughts
and Meditation

BELIEVING FOR A CHILD

God blessed them, and God said to them,
"Be fruitful and multiply; fill the earth...."
Genesis 1:28

So Abraham prayed to God; and God healed
Abimelech, his wife, and his female servants.
Then they bore *children*.
Genesis 20:17

And the LORD visited Sarah as He had said,
and the LORD did for Sarah as He had spoken.
For Sarah conceived and bore Abraham a son
in his old age, at the set time of which God
had spoken to him.
Genesis 21:1, 2

And Sarah said, "God has made me laugh,
and all who hear will laugh with me." She also
said, "Who would have said to Abraham
that Sarah would nurse children?"
Genesis 21:6, 7

"Our sister, *may you become the mother of* thousands
of ten thousands; and may your descendants
possess the gates of those who hate them."
Genesis 24:60

Because you obey the voice of the LORD your God:
...Blessed *shall be* the fruit of your body.
Deuteronomy 28:2, 4

And Elkanah knew Hannah his wife, and the LORD
remembered her. So it came to pass in the process
of time that Hannah conceived and bore a son.
1 Samuel 1:19, 20

"For this child I prayed, and the LORD has granted me my petition which I asked of Him."

1 Samuel 1:27

And Hannah prayed and said: "My heart rejoices in the LORD; my horn is exalted in the LORD."

1 Samuel 2:1

He grants the barren woman a home, like a joyful mother of children. Praise the LORD!

Psalm 113:9

Behold, children *are* a heritage from the LORD, the fruit of the womb *is* a reward. Like arrows in the hand of a warrior, so *are* the children of one's youth.

Psalm 127:3, 4

Your wife *shall be* like a fruitful vine in the very heart of your house, your children like olive plants all around your table.

Psalm 128:3

For You formed my inward parts; You covered me in my mother's womb. I will praise You, for I am fearfully *and* wonderfully made; marvelous are Your works, and *that* my soul knows very well. My frame was not hidden from you, when I was made in secret, *and* skillfully wrought in the lowest parts of the earth. Your eyes saw my substance, being yet unformed. And in Your book they all were written, the days fashioned for me, when *as yet there were* none of them.

Psalm 139:13-16

The LORD has called Me from the womb; from the matrix of My mother He has made mention of My name.

Isaiah 49:1

"Do not be afraid, Zacharias, for your prayer is heard; and your wife Elizabeth will bear you a son."

Luke 1:13

"And you will have joy and gladness, and many will rejoice at his birth. For he will be great in the sight of the Lord."

Luke 1:14, 15

Now after those days his wife Elizabeth conceived; and she hid herself five months, saying, "Thus the Lord has dealt with me, in the days when He looked on *me*, to take away my reproach among people."

Luke 1:24, 25

"Now indeed, Elizabeth your relative has also conceived a son in her old age; and this is now the sixth month for her who was called barren. For with God nothing will be impossible."

Luke 1:36, 37

Now this is the confidence that we have in Him, that if we ask anything according to His will, He hears us.

1 John 5:14

FAITH

Jesus said to him, "If you can believe, all things *are* possible to him who believes."

Mark 9:23

"And whatever things you ask in prayer, believing, you will receive."

Matthew 21:22

Now faith is the substance of things hoped for, the evidence of things not seen.

Hebrews 11:1

But let him ask in faith, with no doubting, for he who doubts is like a wave of the sea driven and tossed by the wind.

James 1:6

But without faith *it is* impossible to please *Him*, for he who comes to God must believe that He is, and *that* He is a rewarder of those who diligently seek Him.

Hebrews 11:6

He did not waver at the promise of God through unbelief, but was strengthened in faith, giving glory to God, and being fully convinced that what He had promised He was also able to perform.

Romans 4:20, 21

VIRTUOUS WOMAN

Who can find a virtuous wife?
For her worth *is* far above rubies.
The heart of her husband safely trusts her;
So he will have no lack of gain.
She does him good and not evil
All the days of her life.
She seeks wool and flax,
And willingly works with her hands.
She is like the merchant ships,
She brings her food from afar.
She also rises while it is yet night,
And provides food for her household,
And a portion for her maidservants.
She considers a field and buys it;
From her profits she plants a vineyard.
She girds herself with strength,
And strengthens her arms.
She perceives that her merchandise *is* good,
And her lamp does not go out by night.

She stretches out her hands to the distaff,
And her hand holds the spindle.
She extends her hand to the poor,
Yes, she reaches out her hands to the needy.
She is not afraid of snow for her household,
For all her household *is* clothed with scarlet.
She makes tapestry for herself;
Her clothing *is* fine linen and purple.
Her husband is known in the gates,
When he sits among the elders of the land.
She makes linen garments and sells *them,*
And supplies sashes for the merchants.
Strength and honor *are* her clothing;
She shall rejoice in time to come.
She opens her mouth with wisdom,
And on her tongue *is* the law of kindness.
She watches over the ways of her household,
And does not eat the bread of idleness.
Her children rise up and call her blessed;
Her husband *also,* and he praises her;
"Many daughters have done well,
But you excel them all."
Charm *is* deceitful and beauty *is* passing,
But a woman *who* fears the LORD, she shall be praised.
Give her of the fruit of her hands,
And let her own works praise her in the gates.

Proverbs 31:10–31

SEEKING COMFORT

Now to Him who is able to do exceedingly
abundantly above all that we ask or think,
according to the power that works in us,
to Him *be* glory in the church by Christ Jesus
to all generations, forever and ever.

Ephesians 3:20, 21

153

Do not cast away your confidence, which has great reward. For you have need of endurance, so that after you have done the will of God, you may receive the promise.

Hebrews 10:35, 36

I will instruct you and teach you in the way you should go.

Psalm 32:8

Trust in the LORD with all your heart, and lean not on your own understanding.

Proverbs 3:5

No evil shall befall you, nor shall any plague come near your dwelling; for He shall give His angels charge over you, to keep you in all your ways.

Psalm 91:10, 11

"Come to Me, all *you* who labor and are heavy laden, and I will give you rest."

Matthew 11:28

SEEKING STRENGTH

I can do all things through Christ who strengthens me.

Philippians 4:13

"Be strong and of good courage, do not fear nor be afraid of them; for the LORD your God, He *is* the One who goes with you. He will not leave you nor forsake you."

Deuteronomy 31:6

"Fear not, for I *am* with you; be not dismayed, for I *am* your God. I will strengthen you, yes, I will help you, I will uphold you with My righteous right hand."

Isaiah 41:10

He gives power to the weak, and to *those who have* no might He increases strength.

Isaiah 40:29

SEEKING PEACE

Be anxious for nothing, but in everything by prayer and supplication, with thanksgiving, let your requests be made known to God; and the peace of God, which surpasses all understanding, will guard your hearts and minds through Christ Jesus.

Philippians 4:6, 7

For God is not *the author* of confusion but of peace, as in all the churches of the saints.

1 Corinthians 14:33

"Peace I leave with you, My peace I give to you; not as the world gives do I give to you. Let not your heart be troubled, neither let it be afraid."

John 14:27

You will keep *him* in perfect peace, *whose* mind *is* stayed on *You,* because he trusts in You.

Isaiah 26:3

Cast your burden on the LORD, and He shall sustain you; He shall never permit the righteous to be moved.

Psalm 55:22

I will both lie down in peace, and sleep; for You alone, O LORD, make me dwell in safety.

Psalm 4:8

HEALING

Bless the LORD, O my soul, and forget not all His benefits: who forgives all your iniquities, who heals all your diseases.

Psalm 103:2, 3

Do not let them depart from your eyes; keep them in the midst of your heart; for they *are* life to those who find them, and health to all their flesh.

Proverbs 4:21, 22

Surely He has borne our griefs and carried our sorrows; yet we esteemed Him stricken, smitten by God, and afflicted. But He *was* wounded for our transgressions, *He was* bruised for our iniquities; the chastisement for our peace *was* upon Him, and by His stripes we are healed.

Isaiah 53:4, 5

He sent His word and healed them, and delivered *them* from their destructions.

Psalm 107:20

Confess *your* trespasses to one another, and pray for one another, that you may be healed.

James 5:16

AGAINST FEAR

For the weapons of our warfare *are* not carnal but mighty in God for pulling down strongholds.

2 Corinthians 10:4

When you lie down, you will not be afraid; yes, you will lie down and your sleep will be sweet. Do not be afraid of sudden terror, nor of trouble from the wicked when it comes; for the LORD will be

your confidence, and will keep your foot from
being caught.

Proverbs 3:24-26

He who dwells in the secret place of the Most High
Shall abide under the shadow of the Almighty.
I will say of the LORD, "*He is* my refuge and my fortress;
My God, in Him I will trust."
Surely He shall deliver you from the snare of the fowler
And from the perilous pestilence.
He shall cover you with His feathers;
And under His wings you shall take refuge;
His truth *shall be your* shield and buckler.
You shall not be afraid of the terror by night,
Nor of the arrow *that* flies by day,
Nor of the pestilence *that* walks in darkness,
Nor of the destruction *that* lays waste at noonday.
A thousand may fall at your side,
And ten thousand at your right hand;
But it shall not come near you.
Only with your eyes shall you look,
And see the reward of the wicked.
Because you have made the LORD, *who* is my refuge,
Even the Most High, your dwelling place,
No evil shall befall you,
Nor shall any plague come near your dwelling;
For He shall give His angels charge over you,
To keep you in all your ways.
In *their* hands they shall bear you up,
Lest you dash your foot against a stone.
You shall tread upon the lion and the cobra,
The young lion and the serpent you shall
    trample underfoot.
"Because he has set his love upon Me, therefore
    I will deliver him;
I will set him on high, because he has known My name.
He shall call upon Me, and I will answer him;

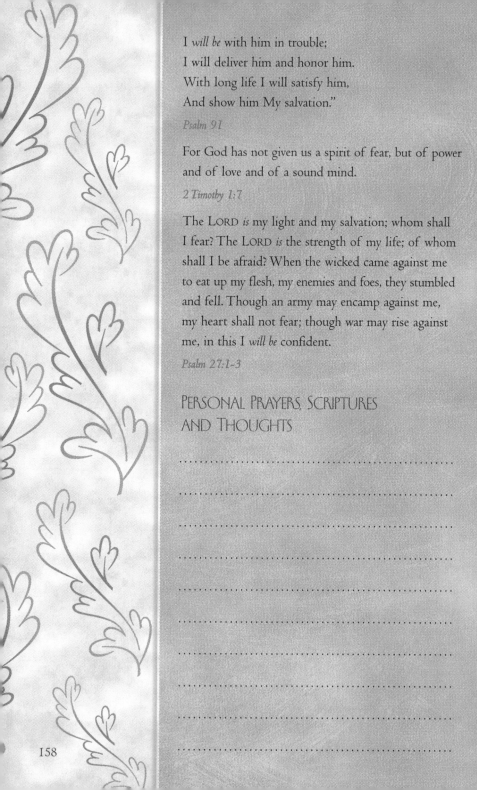

I *will be* with him in trouble;
I will deliver him and honor him.
With long life I will satisfy him,
And show him My salvation."

Psalm 91

For God has not given us a spirit of fear, but of power
and of love and of a sound mind.

2 Timothy 1:7

The LORD *is* my light and my salvation; whom shall
I fear? The LORD *is* the strength of my life; of whom
shall I be afraid? When the wicked came against me
to eat up my flesh, my enemies and foes, they stumbled
and fell. Though an army may encamp against me,
my heart shall not fear; though war may rise against
me, in this I *will be* confident.

Psalm 27:1-3

PERSONAL PRAYERS, SCRIPTURES AND THOUGHTS

....
....
....
....
....
....
....
....
....
....
....

BABY NAMES

A Good Name
is to be Chosen

POSSIBLE BABY NAMES

....

....

....

....

....

....

....

....

....

....

....

....

....

Thus says the LORD, who created you...and He who formed you...
"Fear not, for I have redeemed you; I have called you by your name;
You are Mine."

Isaiah 43:1

ABIGAIL—*Heb.*—father's joy.
Abagael, Abagail, Abbe, Abbey, Abbi, Abbie, Abby, Abbye, Abaigael, Gael, Gail, Gale, Gayle

ABRA—*Heb.*—earth mother; *fem.* of Abraham.

ACACIA—*Gr.*—thorny tree.
Cacia, Cacie, Casey, Casia, Cassie, Kacie, Kasi

ADARA—*Gr.*—beauty; *Ar.*—virgin.
Adra

ADELAIDE—*O.G.*—noble.
Addey, Addi, Addie, Addy, Adel, Adela, Adelaida, Adelais, Adele, Adelheid, Adeline, Adelle, Aline, Del, Della, Delly, Edeline, Heidi

ADENA—*Heb.*—sensuous; decoration.
Adene, Adina, Dena, Dina

ADRIENNE—*Lat.*—from Adria.
Adrea, Adria, Adrian, Adriana, Adriane, Adrianna, Adriena, Hadria

AILEEN—*Ir.*—light; *var.* of Helen.
Aila, Ailee, Ailene, Ailey, Aili, Aleen, Alene, Aline, Eileen, Eleen, Elene, Ileana, Ileane, Ilene, Lena, Lina

AINSLEY—*Gael.*—one's own meadow.
Ainslee, Ainslie, Ansley, Aynslee

AISHA—*Af.*—life; *Ar.*—woman.
Aesha, Asha, Ashia, Asia, Ieasha, Yiesha

AISLINN—*Gael.*—dream.
Ashling, Isleen

ALAMEDA—*Sp.*—poplar tree.

ALANNA—*Gael.*—fair, beautiful; rock.
Alaine, Alana, Alanah, Alane, Alayne, Alleen, Alene, Allina, Allyn, Lana, Lanna

ALBERTA—*O.E.*—noble, shining.
Albertina, Albertine, Ali, Alli, Allie, Ally, Alverta, Auberta, Aubine, Bert, Berta, Berte, Berti, Bertie, Berty, Elberta, Elbertina, Elbertine

ALEXANDRA—*Gr.*—defender of mankind.
Alejandra, Alejandrina, Alessandra, Alex, Alexa, Alexandria, Alexandrina, Alexina, Alexine, Alexis, Ali, Alix, Alla, Alli, Allie, Allix, Ally, Cesya, Elena, Lesya, Lexi, Lexie, Lexine, Lexy, Sande, Sandi, Sandie, Sandra, Sandy, Sandye, Sondra, Zandra

ALICE—*Gr.*—truth; *O.G.*—noble.
Adelice, Ailis, Alecia, Aleece, Ali, Alica, Alicea, Alicen, Alicia, Alika, Alikee, Alis, Alisa, Alisha, Alison, Alissa, Aliz, Alla, Alli, Allie, Allison, Allsun, Allyce, Allys, Alyce, Alys, Alyse, Alysia, Alyss, Alyssa, Elissa, Ilysa, Ilyssa, Licha, Lissa, Lyssa

ALIDA—*Gr.*—beautifully dressed; *Lat.*—small, winged one.
Aleda, Alidia, Alyda, Leda, Lida

ALINA—*Sl.*—bright, beautiful; *Gr.*—light.
Aleen, Alena, Alene, Allene, Lina

ALISON—*Gael.*—little, truthful; *O.G.*—nobility.
Ali, Alie, Alisen, Alisha, Alissa, Alli, Allie, Allison, Allsun, Allyson, Alyson, Alyssa, Lissi, Lissie, Lissy

ALLEGRA—*Lat.*—exuberantly cheerful; joyous.
Allie, Legra

ABBREVIATIONS

Af.	African	*Gr.*	Greek	*M.E.*	Middle English	*O.N.*	Old Norse
Ar.	Arabic	*Heb.*	Hebrew			*Pers.*	Persian
Aram.	Aramaic	*Hin.*	Hindi	*Mus.*	Muslim	*Rus.*	Russian
Celt.	Celtic	*Hun.*	Hungarian	*N.A.*	Native American	*Scan.*	Scandinavian
Dut.	Dutch	*In.*	Indian			*Sl.*	Slavic
Eng.	English	*Ir.*	Irish	*O.D.*	Old Dutch	*Sp.*	Spanish
Fr.	French	*It.*	Italian	*O.E.*	Old English	*Wel.*	Welsh
Gael.	Gaelic	*Jap.*	Japanese	*O.F.*	Old French	*var.*	variation
Ger.	German	*Lat.*	Latin	*O.G.*	Old German		

ALMEDA—*Lat.*—ambitious.
Allmeda, Allmida, Almeta, Almida

ALTA—*Lat.*—high.
Allta

ALYSSA—*Gr.*—sane, rational; alyssum.
Alissa, Allissa, Alysa, Ilyssa, Lyssa

AMANDA—*Lat.*—worthy of love; thoughful and wise.
Amandi, Amandie, Amandy, Manda, Mandi, Mandie, Mandy

AMARA—*Gr.*—eternal beauty.
Amargo, Amarinda, Mara

AMBER—*O.F.*—amber.
Amberetta, Amberly, Ambur

AMELIA—*O.G.*—hard working.
Amalea, Amalee, Amaleta, Amalia, Amalie, Amalija, Amalita, Amelie, Amelina, Ameline, Amelita, Amy, Emelie, Emelina, Emma, Emmy, Mali, Malika, Milly

AMY—*Lat.*—loved; serene in spirit; beloved friend.
Aimee, Amata, Ame, Ami, Amie, Amii, Amye, Esma, Esme

ANASTASIA—*Gr.*—resurrection; springtime.
Ana, Anastasie, Anastassia, Anestassia, Anstice, Asia, Nastassia, Stace, Stacey, Stacie, Stacy, Tasenka, Tasia

ANATOLA—*Gr.*—from the east.

ANDREA—*Lat.*—womanly.
Aindrea, Andee, Anderea, Andra, Andrel, Andi, Andie, Andreana, Andria, Andriana, Andy, Aundrea, Ondrea

ANGELA—*Gr.*—angel, messenger; beautiful one; courageous and admirable—filled with life, radiance and joy.
Aingeal, Ange, Angel, Angele, Angelica, Angelika, Angelina, Angeline, Angelique, Angelita, Angelle, Angie, Angil, Angy, Gelya

ANN, ANNE—*Heb.*—grace, graceful one; faithfully devoted.
Ana, Anet, Anett, Anette, Ania, Anica, Anissa, Anita, Anitra, Anya, Anna, Annabel, Annabella, Annabelle, Anetta, Annie, Annis, Annora, Anny, Anuska, Anya, Hanna, Hannah, Hanni, Hannie, Hanny, Nan, Nana, Nance, Nancee, Nancey, Nanci, Nancie, Nancy, Nanete, Nanette, Nanice, Nanine, Nanni, Nannie, Nanny, Nanon, Netti, Nettie, Netty, Nina, Ninette, Ninon, Nita, Nona

ANTHEA—*Gr.*—like a flower.
Anthe, Anthia, Thia

ANTOINETTE—*Lat.*—priceless; invaluable.
Antonetta, Antonia, Antonie, Antonietta, Antonina, Netta, Netti, Nettie, Netty, Toinette, Toni, Tonia, Tonie, Tony, Tonye

APHRA—*Heb.*—dust; female deer.
Affery, Afra

APRIL—*Lat.*—opening.
Aprilette, Averil, Averyl, Avril

ARABELLA—*Lat.*—beautiful altar; answered prayer.
Ara, Araabela, Arabele, Arabelle, Bel, Bella, Belle

ARDELLE—*Lat.*—burning, enthusiasm.
Arda, Ardeen, Ardelia, Ardelis, Ardella, Ardene, Ardina, Ardis, Ardra

ARDEN—*O.E.*—eagle's valley; *Lat.*—enthusiasm.
Ardenia

ARIADNE—*Gr.*—holy one.
Arene, Ariana, Ariane, Arianie, Ariana

ARIEL—*Heb.*—lioness of God.
Aeriela, Aeriel, Aeriell, Ariela, Ariella, Arielle

ARLENE—*Gael.*—pledge.
Arla, Arlana, Arlee, Arleen, Arlen, Arlena, Arleta, Arlette, Arleyne, Arlie, Arliene, Arlina, Arlinda, Arline, Arluene, Arly, Arlyn, Arlyne, Lena, Lina

ASHLEY—*O.E.*—peaceful spirit of harmony and grace; from the ash tree meadow.
Ashely, Ashla, Ashlee, Ashleigh, Ashlan, Ashlen, Ashli, Ashly

ASTRID—*Scan.*—divine strength; godlike beauty.
Astra

AUBREY—*O.F.*—blond ruler; elf ruler.
Aubree, Aubrette, Aubrie, Aubry
AUDREY—*O.E.*—noble strength.
Audi, Audie, Audra, Audre, Audrie
AUGUSTA—*Lat.*—majestic; respected.
Auguste, Augustina, Augustine,
AVA—*Lat.*—bird.
AVERY—*Lat.*—open to the sun. *var.* of
April.
BARBARA—*Lat.*—stranger, foreigner;
beautiful one, courageous and admirable.
*Bab, Babara, Babb, Babbie, Babette, Babita, Babs,
Barb, Barbe, Barbee, Barbette, Barbey, Barbi,
Barbie, Barbra, Barby*
BEATRICE—*Lat.*—bringer of joy or
happiness.
*Bea, Beatrisa, Beatrix, Bebe, Bee, Beitris, Trix,
Trixie, Trixy*
BELINDA—*Sp.*—beautiful.
Bel, Belle, Linda, Lindie, Lindy
BELLE—*Fr.*—beautiful.
*Belinda, Bell, Bella, Bellina, Belva, Belvia, Bill,
Billi, Billie, Billy*
BENITA—*Lat.*—blessed.
*Bendite, Benedetta, Benedicta, Benedikta, Benetta,
Benni, Bennie, Benny, Benoite, Binni, Binnie,
Binny*
BERYL—*Gr.*—a sea green gemstone.
Berri, Berrie, Berry, Beryle
BETH—*Heb.*—virtuous, tender, and warm;
house of God; *var.* of Elizabeth.
BETHANY—*Aram.*—house of poverty.
Beth, Bethena, Bethina
BETTY—*Heb.*—loyal friend, inspiration to
all; *var.* of Elizabeth.
BEVERLY—*O.E.*—song of harmony and
joy—peaceful, a loving friend; from a
beaver stream or meadow.
*Bev, Beverle, Beverlee, Beverley, Beverlie, Bevvy,
Buffy, Verlee, Verlie*
BIANCA—*It.*—white.
Blanca
BINA—*Af.*—to dance; *Heb.*—wisdom;
knowledge.
Binah, Buna
BLAINE—*Gael.*—slender, lean.
Blane, Blayne

BLAIR—*Gael.*—dweller on the plain.
Blaire
BLAKE—*O.E.*—one with a swarthy
complexion; fair.
Blakelee, Blakeley
BLANCHE—*O.F.*—white; fair.
*Bellanca, Bianca, Blanca, Blanch, Blanka, Blinni,
Blinnie, Blinny*
BLYTHE—*O.E.*—joyous.
Blithe
BONITA—*Sp.*—pretty.
BONNIE—*Gael.*—beautiful one, courageous
and admirable—pure of heart, warm in
spirit.
BRENDA—*O.E.*—fire-brand; burning;
beauty with a noble spirit.
Bren, Brenn
BRENNA—*Gael.*—raven; black-haired.
Bren, Brenn
BRETT—*Gael.*—from Britain.
Britt
BRIANA—*Gael.*—strong; hill.
*Brana, Breana, Breanne, Breena, Bria,
Brianna, Brianne, Brina, Briney, Brinn,
Brinna, Briny, Bryana, Bryn, Bryna,
Brynn, Brynne*
BRIDGET—*Gael.*—powerful; strength.
*Beret, Berget, Biddie, Biddy, Birgit, Birgitta, Bride,
Bridgette, Bridie, Brietta, Brigid, Brigida, Brigit,
Brigitta, Brigitte, Brita*
BRITTANY—*Lat.*—from England; generosity
of spirit, gracious and kind.
*Brit, Britney, Britni, Britt, Britta, Brittan,
Brittaney, Brittani, Britteny, Brittnee, Brittney,
Brittni*
BRONWYN—*Wel.*—white breast.
BROOKE—*O.E.*—small stream.
BRYN—*Wel.*—mount.
Brynna, Brynne
CAITLIN—*Wel.*—*var.* of Catherine
CALLA—*Gr.*—beautiful.
CAMILLE—*Lat.*—young ceremonial
attendant; messenger.
*Cam, Camala, Camel, Cami, Camila, Camile,
Cammilla, Cammi, Cammie, Cammy, Milli,
Millie, Milly*
CANDACE, CANDICE—*Gr.*—glittering;
brilliantly white.

Candi, Candie, Candis, Candy, Kandace, Kandy

CARA—*Gael.*—friend; *Lat.*—dear, darling.

Caralie, Carina, Carine, Carrie, Kara

CARINA—*Lat.*—keel; *It.*—dear little one.

Carena, Carin, Carine, Caryn, Karena,
Karina, Karine

CARISSA—*Gr.*—loving; grace.

Caresa, Caressa, Carrissa, Charissa, Karisa,
Karissa

CARMEL—*Heb.*—garden.

Carma, Carmela, Carmelina, Carmelita, Lita

CARMEN—*Lat.*—song; *Sp.*—from Mt. Carmel.

Carma, Carmelina, Carmelita, Carmencita,
Carmina, Carmine, Carmita, Charmaine,
Karmen

CAROL—*Lat.*—strong; womanly; spirit-
filled, compassionate; *O.F.*—song of joy.

Carry, Cari, Carla, Carleen, Carlen, Carlene,
Carley, Carlin, Carlina, Carline, Carlita, Carlota,
Carlotta, Carly, Carlyn, Carlynn, Carlynne, Caro,
Carola, Carole, Carolyn, Carolynn, Carolynne,
Carri, Carrie, Carroll, Carry, Cary, Caryl, Charla,
Charleen, Charlena, Charlene, Charlotta, Charmain,
Charmaine, Charmain, Charmion, Charyl, Cheryl,
Cherlyn, Karel, Kari, Karla, Karleen, Karlen,
Karlene, Karlotta, Karlotte, Karole, Karolina,
Karoly, Karyl, Kerril, Lola, Loleta, Lolita,
Lotta, Lotte, Lotti, Lottie, Sharleen, Sharlene,
Sharline, Sharyl, Sherrie, Sherry, Sherye,
Sheryl

CAROLINE, CAROLYN—*Lat.*—little and
womanly.

Carla, Carleen, Carlen, Carlene, Carley, Carlin,
Carlina, Carline, Carlita, Carlota, Carlotta,
Carly, Carlyn, Carlynn, Carlynne, Carol, Carola,
Carole, Carolin, Carolina, Carolyne, Carolynn,
Carolynne, Carri, Carrie, Carroll, Cary, Charla,
Charleen, Charlena, Charlene, Karla, Karleen,
Karlen, Karlene, Karolina, Karolyn

CASEY—*Gael.*—brave; watchful.

Casi, Casie, Kacey, Kacie, Kacy, Kasey, Kaycee

CASSANDRA—*Gr.*—helper or defender of
men; disbelieved by men.

Casandra, Cass, Cassandre, Cassandry,
Cassaundra, Cassi, Cassie, Cassondra, Cassy,
Kassandra, Sandi, Sandie, Sandy, Saundra, Sondra

CATHERINE—*Gr.*—pure.

Caitlin, Caitrin, Caren, Cari, Carin, Caron,
Caryn, Cass, Cassi, Cassie, Cassy, Catarina,
Caterina, Catha, Catharina, Catharine, Cathleen,
Cathlene, Cathyleen, Cathrine, Cathryn, Catina,
Catlaina, Catrina, Catriona, Ekaterina

CATHY—*var.* of Catherine.

Cathe, Cathee, Cathi, Cathie

CECILIA—*Lat.*—blind.

Cacila, Cacilie, Cecil, Cecile, Ceciley, Cecily, Ceil,
Cele, Celia, Celie, Cicely, Cicily, Ciel, Cilka,
Cissie, Cissy, Kikelia, Sile, Sileas, Sisely, Sisile,
Sissie, Sissy

CELESTE—*Lat.*—heavenly.

Cele, Celesta, Celestia, Celestina, Celestine,
Celestyn, Celestyna, Celia, Celie, Celina, Celinda,
Celine, Celinka, Celisse, Celka, Selestina

CHANDRA—*In.*—moonlike.

Shandra

CHARITY—*Lat.*—charity, brotherly love.

Carissa, Carita, Charis, Charissa, Charita,
Cherri, Cherry, Sharity

CHARLOTTE—*Fr.*—little and womanly.

Carla, Carleen, Carlene, Carline, Carlota,
Carlotta, Carly, Chara, Charil, Charla, Charleen,
Charlene, Charline, Charlotta, Charmain,
Charmaine, Charmian, Charmion, Charo, Karla,
Karleen, Karlene, Karlotta, Karlotte, Lola, Loleta,
Lolita, Lotta, Lotte, Lotti, Lottie, Sharleen, Sharlene,
Sharline, Sherrie, Sherry, Sherye

CHELSEA—*O.E.*—a port; landing.

Chelsae, Chelsey, Chelsie, Chelsy, Cheslie

CHERYL—*var.* of Charlotte.

CHLOE—*Gr.*—green, young plant.

CHRISTINE—*Gr.*—devoted friend, inspired
by love; Christian; anointed.

Cairistiona, Cristen, Crystie, Chris, Chrissie,
Chrissy, Christa, Christan, Christel, Christean,
Christen, Christi, Christian, Christiana,
Christiane, Christie, Christin, Christina, Christy,
Christye, Christyna, Chrysta, Chrystal, Chryste,
Cris, Crissie, Crissy, Crista, Cristi, Cristie,
Cristin, Cristina, Cristine, Cristiona, Cristy,
Crystal, Kirsten

CINDY—*Gr.*—radiant spirit, filled with
love; *var.* of Cynthia.

CLARA—*Gr.*—clear, bright.

Chiarra, Clair, Claire, Clarabelle, Clare, Claresta,
Clareta, Claretta, Clarette, Clarey, Clari, Clarice,
Clarie, Clarinda, Clarine, Clarissa, Clarita,

Clary, Klara, Klarika, Klarrisa

CLAUDIA—*Lat.*–lame.

*Claude, Claudelle, Claudetta, Claudette, Claudie,
Claudina, Claudine, Gladys*

CODY—*O.E.*–a cushion or pillow.

Codee, Codi, Codie

COLETTE—*Gr./Fr.*–victorious.

Collette, Coletta, Collette

COLLEEN—*Gael.*–girl.

Coleen, Colene, Collie, Colline

CONNIE—*var.* of Constance.

Con, Connie, Conny

CONSTANCE—*Lat.*–constancy, firmness.

*Constancia, Constancy, Constanta, Constantia,
Constantina, Constantine, Costanza, Konstance*

CONSUELO—*Sp.*–consolation or comfort.

Consolata, Consuela

CORDELIA—*Wel.*–jewel of the sea;
Lat.–from the heart.

*Cordelie, Cordey, Cordi, Cordie, Cordula, Cordy,
Delia, Kordula*

COREY—*Gael.*–from a hollow.

*Cory, Cori, Corie, Correy, Corri, Corrie, Corry,
Kori, Korrie, Korry*

CORNELIA—*Lat.*–yellow; hornlike.

*Cornela, Cornelle, Cornie, Corny,
Neely, Nelia, Nelie, Nell, Nellie,
Nelly*

COURTNEY—*O.E.*–from the court.

Cortney, Courtenay, Courtnay, Korney

CYNTHIA—*Gr.*–moon; moon goddess.

*Cinda, Cindee, Cindi, Cindie, Cindy, Cynde,
Cyndia, Cyndie, Cynthea, Cynthie, Cynthy,
Kynthia, Sindee*

DACEY—*Gael.*–southerner.

Dacia, Dacie, Dacy, Dasi, Dasie

DAHLIA—*Scan.*–from the valley; for the
dahlia flower.

Dalia

DAISY—*O.E.*–eye of the day; daisy.

Daisey, Daisi, Daisie

DALE—*O.E.*–from the valley.

Dael, Daile, Dayle

DAMITA—*Sp.*–little noble woman.

DANA—*Scan.*–from Denmark.

Dayna, Tana

DANIELLE—*Heb.*–judged by God;

warm-hearted, generous in spirit.

*Danella, Danelle, Danette, Dani, Danice, Daniela,
Daniele, Daniella, Danila, Danit, Danita, Danna,
Danni, Dannie, Danny, Dannye, Danya, Danyelle*

DAPHNE—*Gr.*–laurel tree.

Daffi, Daffie, Daffy, Daphna

DARA—*Heb.*–compassion; wisdom.

Darda, Darya

DARBY—*Gael.*–free man; *O.N.*–from the
deer park.

Darb, Darbee, Darbie, Derby

DARCY—*Gael.*–dark; *O.F.*–from Arcy.

D'Arcy, Dar, Darce, Darcie, Darice, Darsey

DARLENE—*O.F.*–little darling.

*Dareen, Darelle, Darla, Darleen, Darline,
Darlleen, Darrelle, Darryl, Daryl*

DAVITA—*Heb.*–beloved.

*Daveen, Daveta, Davida, Davina, Davine, Devina,
Veda, Vida, Vita, Vitia*

DAWN—*O.E.*–shining light, full of joy.

DEBBIE—*Heb.*–compassionate leader,
respected and admired; *var.* of Deborah.

DEBORAH—*Heb.*–bee.

*Deb, Debbee, Debbi, Debbie, Debby, Debi, Debor,
Debora, Debra, Devora*

DEIRDRE—*Gael.*–sorrow; fear; complete
wanderer.

*Dede, Dedra, Dee, DeeDee, Deerdre, Deidre, Didi,
Dierdre*

DELANEY—*Gael.*–offspring of the challenger.

Delanie

DELIA—*Gr.*–visible; from Delos.

*Dee, Dede, DeeDee, Dehlia, Dela, Delinda, Della,
Didi*

DEMETRIA—*Gr.*–belonging to or follower
of Demeter.

Demeter, Demetra, Demetris

DENA—*Heb.*–vindicated; *O.E.*–from the
valley.

*Deana, Deane, Deanna, Deena, Deeyn, Dene,
Denna, Denni, Dina*

DENISE—*Fr.*–follower of Dionysus.

*Deni, Denice, Denni, Dennie, Denny, Denys,
Denyse, Dinnie, Dinny*

DIANA—*Lat.*–divine.

*Deana, Deane, Deanna, Deanne, Dede, Dee, DeeDee,
Dena, Di, Diahann, Dian, Diandra, Diane,
Dianna, Dianne, Didi, Dyan, Dyana, Dyane,*

Dyann, Dyanna, Dyanne

DIANE—*Lat.*—blessed one of beauty and splendor; divine; *var.* of Diana.

DIONNE—*Gr.*—divine queen; follower of Dionysius.
Deonne, Dion, Dione, Dionis.

DIXIE—*Fr.*—ten, tenth.
Dix

DOLORES—*Sp.*—sorrows.
Delora, Delores, Deloria, Deloris, Dolorita, Doloritas, Lola, Lolita

DOMINIQUE—*Fr./Lat.*—belonging to God.
Domeniga, Dominga, Domini, Dominica

DONNA—*Lat./It.*—honorable lady; gracious and pure.
Doña, Donella, Donelle, Donetta, Donia, Donica, Donielle, Donnell, Donni, Donnie, Donny, Ladonna

DORA—*Gr.*—gift.
Dode, Dodi, Dodie, Dody, Doralia, Doralin, Doralyn, Doralynn, Doralynne, Dore, Doreen, Dorelia, Dorella, Dorelle, Dorena, Dorene, Doretta, Dorette, Dorey, Dori, Dorie, Dorita, Doro, Dorree, Dory

DOREEN—*Gael.*—sullen; *Fr.*—gilded.
Dorene, Dorine

DORIS—*Gr.*—from the sea; from Doris.
Dori, Doria, Dorice, Dorisa, Dorise, Dorita, Dorri, Dorrie, Dorris, Dorry, Dory

DOROTHY—*Gr.*—gift of God.
Dasha, Dasya, Dode, Dody, Doe, Doll, Dolley, Dolli, Dollie, Dolly, Dora, Dori, Dorlisa, Doro, Dorolice, Dorotea, Doroteya, Dorothea, Dorothée, Dorthea, Dorthy, Dory, Dosi, Dot, Dotti, Dottie, Dotty

DRUSILLA—*Lat.*—descendant of Drusus, the strong one.
Drew, Dru, Druci, Drucie, Drucill, Drucy, Drusi, Drusie, Drusy

DYLANA—*Wel.*—from the sea.
Dylane

EARTHA—*O.E.*—of or from the earth.
Erda, Ertha, Herta, Hertha

EDEN—*Heb.*—delight, pleasure.
Edin

EDITH—*O.E.*—rich gift; prosperity.
Dita, Eadith, Eadie, Eda, Ede, Edi, Edie, Edita, Editha, Edithe, Ediva, Edy, Edyth, Edythe, Eyde,

Eydie

EDWINA—*O.E.*—rich friend.

EILEEN—*Ir.*—shining; *var.* of Helen.
Ailene, Eiley, Ilene, Leana, Lina

ELAINE—*O.F.*—bright; *var.* of Helen.
Alaina, Alayne, Elana, Elayne, Ellane, Laine, Layney

ELEANOR—*Gr.*—light.
Eleanora, Eleanore, Elenore, Ella, Elladine, Elle, Ellen, Ellene, Elli, Ellie, Elly, Ellyn, Elna, Elnora, Leanora, Lena, Lenora, Lenore, Leonora, Leonore, Leora, Nell, Nellie, Nelly, Nora

ELECTRA—*Gr.*—shining, brilliant.

ELIZABETH—*Heb.*—oath of God; pledged to God; great character, dedicated and true.
Belita, Belle, Bess, Bessie, Bessy, Beth, Betsey, Betsy, Beta, Bette, Betti, Bettina, Bettine, Betty, Ealasaid, Eilis, Elisa, Elisabet, Elisabeth, Elisabetta, Elise, Elissa, Eliza, Elizabet, Elsa, Elsbeth, Else, Elsey, Elsi, Elsie, Elspet, Elspeth, Elsy, Elyse, Helsa, Isabel, Lib, Libbey, Libbi, Libbie, Libby, Lisa, Lisabeth, Lisbeth, Lise, Lisette, Lissa, Lissie, Lissy, Liz, Liza, Lizabeth, Lizbeth, Lizzie, Lizzy, Lusa, Ysabel

ELLEN—*Eng.*—*var.* of Helen.
Ellene, Ellie, Elly, Ellyn

ELSA—*O.G.*—noble.
Else, Elsie, Elsy, Ilsa, Ilse

ELVIRA—*Ger./Sp.*—elf-counsel; excelling.
Elva, Elvera, Elvina, Elwira, Lira

EMILY—*O.G.*—industrious; *Lat.*—winning spirit, filled with happiness.
Aimil, Amalea, Amalia, Amalie, Amelia, Amélie, Ameline, Amelita, Amy, Eimile, Em, Emalee, Emalia, Emelda, Emelia, Emelina, Emeline, Emelita, Emelyne, Emera, Emilee, Emili, Emilia, Emilie, Emiline, Emlyn, Emlynn, Emlynne, Emmalee, Emmaline, Emmalyn, Emmalynn, Emmalynne, Emmey, Emmi, Emmie, Emmy, Emmye, Emyle, Emylee, Milka

EMMA—*O.G.*—universal; everything; nurse.
Em, Ema, Emelina, Emeline, Emelyne, Emmaline, Emmalyn, Emmalynn, Emmalynne, Emmi, Emmie, Emmy, Emmye

ENID—*Wel.*—purity; woodlark; life.
Eanid, Enyd

ERICA—*Scan.*—all-ruler; ever-powerful.

ERIN—*Gael.*—peace; from Ireland; faithful friend, warm and gentle.

Aaren, Aaryn, Eran, Erina, Erinne, Erinna, Eryn

ERLINE—*O.E.*–elfin girl.

ERNESTINE—*O.E.*–earnest; sincere.

Erna, Ernaline, Ernesta

EUDORA—*Gr.*–honored gift.

Dora

EUGENIA—*Gr.*–well born.

Eugénie, Gene, Genia, Janie, Jenna

EVANGELINE—*Gr.*–bearer of good news.

Eva, Evangelia, Evangelina, Eve

EVE—*Heb.*–life.

Eba, Ebba, Eva, Evaleen, Evelina, Eveline, Evelyn, Evey, Evie, Evita, Evonne, Evvie, Evvy, Evy

FAITH—*M.E.*–fidelity; loyalty.

Fae, Fay, Faye, Fath, Faythe

FALLON—*Gael.*–descendant of the ruler.

FARRAH—*M.E.*–beautiful; pleasant.

Fara, Faraha, Farand, Farra, Farrand, Fayre

FATIMA—*Ar.*–unknown.

Fatimah, Fatma

FAY—*O.F.*–fairy; elf.

Fae, Faye, Fayette, Fayina

FELICIA—*Lat.*–happy; lucky.

Felecia, Felice, Felicidad, Félicie, Felicity, Félise, Felisha, Felita, Feliza

FIONA—*Gael.*–fair, pale.

Fionna

FIONNULA—*Gael.*–white-shouldered.

Fenella, Finella

FLANNERY—*O.F.*–a flat piece of metal.

Flan, Flann, Flanna

FLEUR—*Fr.*–flower.

FLORENCE—*Lat.*–blooming; prosperous.

Fiorenza, Flo, Flor, Flora, Florance, Florie, Florina, Florinda, Florine, Floris, Florri, Florrie, Florry, Floss, Flossi, Flossie, Flossy

FRANCES—*Lat.*–free; from France.

Fan, Fanchette, Fanchon, Fancie, Fannie, Fanny, Fanya, Fran, Francesca, Franci, Francie, Francine, Francisca, Franciska, Francoise, Francyne, Frank, Frankie, Franky, Franni, Frannie, Franny

FREDA—*O.G.*–peaceful.

Frayda, Fredella, Freida, Frieda

FREDERICA—*O.G.*–peaceful ruler.

Farica, Federica, Fred, Freddi, Freddie, Freddy, Fredericka, Frédérique, Fredia, Fredra, Fredrika, Friederike, Rica, Ricki, Rickie, Ricky, Rikki

FREYA—*Scan.*–noble woman; the goddess Freya.

Fraya

GABRIELLE—*Heb.*–God is my strength; God's heroine.

Gabbey, Gabbi, Gabbie, Gabey, Gabi, Gabie, Gabriel, Gabriela, Gabriell, Gabriella, Gabriellia, Gabrila, Gaby, Gavra, Gavrielle

GAIL—*O.E.*–gay, lively; my father's joy.

Gael, Gale, Gayla, Gale, Gayleen, Gaylene

GEMMA—*Lat./It.*–jewel, precious stone.

Jemma

GENEVA—*O.F.*–juniper tree.

Gena, Genevra, Janeva

GENEVIEVE—*O.G./Fr.*–white wave.

Gena, Geneva, Geneviève, Genevra, Gennie, Genny, Genovera, Gina, Janeva, Jennie, Jenny

GEORGIA—*Lat.*–farmer.

George, Georgeanna, Georgeanne, Georgena, Georgetta, Georgette, Georgiana, Georgianna

GERALDINE—*O.G.*–spearruler.

Géraldine, Gerhardine, Geri, Gerianna, Gerianne, Gerri, Gerrie, Gerrilee, Gerry, Girald, Jeralee, Jere, Jeri, Jerrie, Jerry

GILDA—*O.E.*–covered with gold.

GILLIAN—*Lat.*–*fem.* of Julian.

GINGER—*Lat.*–the ginger flower or spice; var. of Virginia.

GISELLE—*O.G.*–pledge; hostage.

Gisela, Gisele, Gisella, Gizela

GLENNA—*Gael.*–from the valley or glen.

Glenda, Glenine, Glen, Glenn, Glennie, Glennis, Glyn, Glynis, Glynnis

GLORIA—*Lat.*–glory.

Gloree, Glori, Gloriana, Glory

GUINEVERE—*Wel.*–white, fair; white wave.

Freddi, Freddie, Freddy, Fredi, Gaynor, Genevieve, Genna, Genni, Gennie, Gennifer, Genny, Ginevra, Guenevere, Guenna, Guinna, Gwen, Gwenora, Gwenore, Janifer, Jen, Jenifer, Jennee, Jenni, Jennie, Jennifer, Jenny, Ona, Oona, Una, Winifred, Winni, Winnie, Winny

GWENDOLYN—*Wel.*–white; white-browed.

Guendolen, Guenna, Gwen, Gwendolen, Gwendolin, Gwenette, Gwenni, Gwennie, Gwenny, Gwyn, Gwyneth, Gwynne, Wendi, Wendie, Wendy, Wynne

GWYNETH—*Wel.*–white; blessed; happiness.

Gwynne, Winnie, Winny, Wynne, Wynnie, Wynny
HALEY—*Scan.*—hero.
Hailee, Haily, Haleigh, Halie, Hally, Hayley
HANNAH—*Heb.*—graceful.
Hana, Hanna, Hanni, Hannie, Hanny, Honna
HARLEY—*O.E.*—a long field.
Arlea, Arley, Harlene, Harli, Harlie
HARRIET—*O.F.*—ruler of the home.
Harri, Harrie, Harrietta, Harriette, Harriot, Harriott, Hatti, Hattie, Hatty
HEATHER—*M.E.*—flowering heather; one who moves with kindness.
HELEN—*Gr.*—light.
Aila, Aileen, Ailene, Aleen, Eileen, Elaine, Elana, Elane, Elayne, Eleanor, Eleanore, Eleen, Elena, Elene, Eleni, Elenore, Eleonora, Eleonore, Elianora, Elinor, Elinore, Ella, Elladine, Elle, Ellen, Ellene, Ellette, Elli, Ellie, Elly, Ellyn, Ellynn, Elna, Elnora, Elora, Elyn
HILARY—*Gr.*—cheerful.
Hillary, Hilliary
HONORA—*Lat.*—honorable.
Honey, Honor, Honoria, Honorine
ILONA—*Hun.*—beautiful; *var.* of Helen; *Gk.*—Light.
Ilonka
IMOGENE—*Lat.*—image.
Emogene, Imogen, Imojean
INGRID—*Scan.*—hero's daughter; beautiful.
Inga, Ingaberg, Ingaborg, Inge, Ingeberg, Inger, Ingunna
IOLA—*Gr.*—cloud of dawn.
IONE—*Gr.*—violet-colored stone.
Iona
ISABEL—*Sp.*—consecrated to God.
Belia, Belicia, Belita, Bell, Bella, Belle, Ib, Ibbie, Ibby, Isa, Isabeau, Isabelita, Isabella, Isabelle, Iseabal, Isobel, Issi, Issie, Issy, Izabel, Ysabel
ISADORA—*Lat.*—gift of Isis.
Isidora
IVY—*O.E.*—ivy tree.
Ivie
JANE—*Heb.*—gift of grace.
JANET—*var.* of Jane.
JEAN—*Scot.*—*var.* of Jane
JENNIFER—*var.* of Genevieve.
JILL—*Dut.*—most clever one.

JOAN—*Heb.*—*fem.* of John.
JOCELYN—*Lat.*—merry; *O.E.*—just.
JOELLE—*Heb.*—Jehovah is Lord; the Lord is willing.
JOLENE—*M.E.*—he will increase.
Joleen, Joline, Jolyn
JOLIE—*Fr.*—pretty.
Jolee, Joli, Joly
JORDAN—*Heb.*—descending.
Jordain, Jordana, Jordanna, Jorey, Jori, Jorie, Jorrie, Jorry, Jourdan
JOSEPHINE—*Heb.*—he shall increase.
Fifi, Fifine, Fina, Jo, Joette, Joey, Joline, Josee, Josefa, Josefina, Josepha, Josephina, Josey, Josi, Josie, Josy
JOYCE—*Lat.*—joyous.
Joice, Joyous
JUDITH—*Heb.*—of Judah; Jewish.
Giuditta, Jodi, Jodie, Jody, Judi, Judie, Juditha, Judy, Judye
JUDY—*Heb.*—wise and honorable, an inspiration to all; *var.* of Judith.
JULIA—*Lat.*—youthful.
Giulia, Jiulietta, Joletta, Julee, Juli, Juliana, Juliane, Juliann, Julianne, Julie, Julienne, Juliet, Julieta, Julietta, Juliette, Julina, Juline, Julissa, Julita
JULIE—*Lat.*—young in spirit, guided by truth; *var.* of Julia.
JUSTINE—*Lat.*—just; righteous.
Giustina, Justina, Justinn
KATHERINE—*Gr.*—pure.
Caitlin, Caitrin, Caren, Carin, Caron, Caryn, Cass, Cassie, Cassy, Catarina, Cate, Caterina, Catha, Catharina, Catharine, Cathe, Cathee, Caterina, Catherine, Cathi, Cathie, Cathleen, Cathlene, Cathrine, Cathryn, Cathy, Cati, Catie, Catlaina, Catriona, Cathyleen, Caty, Caye, Ekaterina, Kakalina, Karen, Karena, Kari, Karin, Karna, Kass, Kassi, Kassia, Kassie, Kata, Katalin, Kate, Katerina, Katerine, Katey, Kath, Katha, Katharine, Katharyn, Kathe, Katheryn, Kathi, Kathie, Kathleen, Kathryn, Katheryne, Kathy, Kathye, Katie, Katina, Katinka, Katrina, Katrine
KAREN—*Gr.*—warm-hearted, pure and beloved; *var.* of Katherine.
KATHY—*Gr.*—admired one, true and pure; *var.* of Katherine.

KEELY—*Gael.*—beautiful; var. of Kelly.
Keeley, Keelia
KEIKO—*Jap.*—adored.
KEISHA—*Unknown.*
KELLY—*Gael.*—trustworthy friend, loyal and true; warrior woman.
Kelley, Kellen, Kelli, Kellia, Kellie, Kellina
KELSEY—*Scan.*—from the ship island.
Kelcey, Kelci, Kelcie, Kelcy, Kellsie, Kelsi, Kelsy, Kesley, Keslie
KENDRA—*O.E.*—knowledgeable.
Kendre, Kenna, Kinna
KERRY—*Gael.*—dark; dark-haired.
Keri, Keriann, Kerianne, Kerri, Kerrie
KESIA—*Af.*—favorite.
Kessiah, Kissee, Kissiah, Kissie, Kizzee, Kizzie
KIAH—*Af.*—season's beginning.
Ki
KIM—*O.E.*—guiding spirit, full of grace; var. of Kimberly.
KIMBERLY—*O.E.*—from the royal fortress meadow.
Cymbre, Kim, Kimberlee, Kimberley, Kimberli, Kimberlyn, Kimbra, Kimmi, Kimmie, Kimmy, Kym
KIRA—*Pers.*—sun.
KIRBY—*O.E.*—from the church town.
Kirbee, Kirbie
KORA—*Gr.*—maiden.
Cora, Corabel, Corabella, Corabelle, Corella, Corena, Corene, Coretta, Corette, Corey, Cori, Corie, Corina, Corinna, Corinne, Coriss, Corissa, Corrina, Corrine, Corry, Kore, Korella, Koren, Koressa, Kori, Korie
KYLE—*Gael.*—handsome; living near the chapel; narrow slice of land.
Kial, Kiele, Kiley, Kyla, Kylen, Kylie, Kylynn
LANE—*M.E.*—from the narrow road.
Laina, Laney, Lanie, Lanni, Lanny, Layne
LARA—*Lat.*—shining; famous.
LARAINE—*Lat.*—sea bird; gull.
Larina, Larine
LAURA—*Lat.*—virtuous one of beauty and wisdom; crown of laurel.
Lari, Lauralee, Lauré, Laureen, Laurel, Laurella, Lauren, Laurena, Laurene, Lauretta, Laurette, Lauri, Laurice, Laurie, Lora, Loree, Loreen, Loren,

Lorena, Lorene, Lorenza, Loretta, Lorette, Lori, Lorinda, Lorita, Lorna, Lorri, Lorrie, Lorry
LAUREN—*Lat.*—kind, gentle and creative; var. of Laura.
LAVEDA—*Lat.*—cleansed.
LAVERNE—*O.F.*—from the grove of alder trees; *Lat.*—springlike.
Laverna, LaVerne, Verna
LAVINIA—*Lat.*—purified; Roman women.
Lavena, Lavina, Lavinie, Vin, Vinni, Vinnie, Vinny
LEAH—*Heb.*—weary.
Lea, Lee, Leia, Leigh, Leigha, Lia
LEANDRA—*Lat.*—like a lion.
Leandra, Leodora, Leoine, Leoline, Leonanie, Leonelle
LEE—*Gael.*—poetic; *O.E.*—from the pasture meadow.
Leann, Leanna, Leeann, Leeanne, LeeAnn, Leigh
LEILA—*Ar.*—dark as night.
Layla, Leela, Leelah, Leilah, Lela, Lelah, Leland, Lelia, Leyla
LENA—*Lat.*—temptress.
Lenee, Lenette, Lina, Lynée
LEONA—*Lat.*—lion.
Leoine, Leola, Leone, Leonelle, Léonie.
LESLIE—*Gael.*—from the gray fortress.
Leslee, Lesley, Lesli, Lesly, Lezlie
LETITIA—*Lat.*—joy.
Laetitia, Latashia, Latia, Latisha, Latreshia, Latrice, Leda, Leisha, Leshia, Let, Leta, Lethia, Leticia, Letisha, Letizia, Letta, Letti, Lettie, Letty, Loutitia, Tish, Tisha
LIDA—*Sl.*—beloved of the people.
Lyda
LILITH—*Ar.*—of the night; ghost.
Lillis, Lilly, Lily
LILLIAN—*Lat.*—lily flower.
Lil, Lila, Lilas, Lili, Lilia, Lilian, Liliane, Lilias, Lilla, Lilli, Lillie, Lilly, Lily, Lilyan, Liuka
LINDA—*Sp.*—pretty, virtuous one of beauty and wisdom.
Lind, Lindi, Lindie, Lindy, Lynda, Lynde, Lyndy
LINDSAY, LINDSEY—*O.E.*—from the linden tree island.
Lind, Lindsy, Linzy, Lyndsay, Lyndsey, Lyndsie, Lynsey
LINETTE—*Celt.*—graceful; *O.F.*—linnet.
Lanette, Linet, Linnet, Lynette, Lynnet, Lynnette

LINNEA—*Scan.*—lime or linden tree.
Linea, Lynea, Lynnea
LISA—*Heb.*—dedicated friend, witness to truth; *var.* of Elizabeth.
LORELEI—*Ger.*—alluring.
Loralee, Loralie, Loralyn, Lorilee, Lorilyn, Lura, Lurette, Lurleen, Lurlene, Lurline
LORI—*Lat.*—honorable friend, crowned with dignity; *var.* of Laura.
LORRAINE—*Fr.*—from Lorraine.
Laraine, Lorain, Loraine, Lori, Lorine, Lorrayne
LOUISE—*O.G.*—famous woman warrior.
Alison, Allison, Aloise, Aloisia, Aloysia, Eloisa, Eloise, Héloise, Lois, Loise, Lola, Lolita, Lou, Louisa, Louisette, Loyce, Lu, Ludovika, Luisa, Luise, Lulita, Lulu
LUCY—*Lat.*—light; light-bringer.
Lu, Luce, Luci, Lucia, Luciana, Lucie, Lucienne, Lucilla, Lucille, Lucina, Lucinda, Lucine, Lucita, Luz
LYDIA—*Gr.*—from Lydia.
Lidia, Lydie
LYNN—*O.E.*—waterfall; pool below a fall.
Lin, Linell, Linn, Linnell, Lyn, Lyndell, Lynée, Lynelle, Lynette, Lynna, Lynne, Lynnell, Lynnelle, Lynnett, Lynnette
MABEL—*Lat.*—lovable.
Amabel, Mab, Mabelle, Mable, Maible, Maybelle
MACKENZIE—*Gael.*—son of the wise leader.
Kenzie
MADELINE—*Gr.*—woman from Magdala.
Dalenna, Lena, Lenna, Lina, Linn, Lynn, Lynne, Mada, Madalena, Madalyn, Maddalena, Maddi, Maddie, Maddy, Madel, Madelaine, Madeleine, Madelena, Madelene, Madelina, Madella, Madelle, Madelon, Madge, Madlen, Madlin, Mady, Magda, Magdala, Magdalena, Magdalene, Maidel, Maighdlin, Mala, Malena, Malina, Marleah, Marleen, Marlena, Marlene, Marline, Maud, Maude
MAEVE—*Gael.*—delicate, fragile.
MAHALIA—*Heb.*—affection.
Mahala, Mahelia
MAIA—*Gr.*—mother or nurse.
Maiah, Maya, Mya
MALLORY—*O.G.*—army counselor; *O.F.*—unhappy.
Mal, Mallorie, Malorie, Malory

MANUELA—*Sp.*—God is with us.
MARCELLA—*Lat.*—belonging to Mars; warlike.
Marcela, Marcelle, Marcellina, Marcelline, Marchelle, Marcile, Marcille, Marcy, Marquita, Marsiella
MARCIA—*Lat.*—warlike.
Marcelia, Marcie, Marcile, Marcille, Marcy, Marquita, Marsha
MARGARET—*Gr.*—genuine treasure blessed with love; pearl.
Greta, Gretal, Gretchen, Gretel, Grethel, Gretta, Madge, Mag, Maggi, Maggie, Maggy, Maiga, Maisie, Marcheta, Marga, Margalo, Margareta, Marge, Margery, Marjorie, Marjory, Marketa, Meg, Megan, Meggi, Meggie, Meggy, Meghan, Meta, Peg, Pegeen, Peggi, Peggie, Peggy, Rita
MARIE—*Fr. var.* of Mary.
MARILYN—*var.* of Mary.
MARIS—*Lat.*—of the sea.
Marisa, Marissa, Marris, Marys, Meris
MARTHA—*Aram.*—lady.
Marta, Martelle, Marthe, Marthena, Marti, Martie, Martina, Martita, Marty, Martynee, Matti, Mattie, Matty, Pat, Patti, Pattie, Patty
MARY—*Heb.*—blessed one, pure in heart; bitter.
Mair, Maire, Malia, Mame, Mamie, Manon, Manya, Mara, Marabel, Maren, Maria, Mariam, Marian, Marianna, Marianne, Marice, Maridel, Marie, Mariel, Marietta, Marilee, Marilin, Marilyn, Marin, Marion, Mariquilla, Mariska, Marita, Maritsa, Marja, Marje, Marla, Marlo, Marnia, Marya, Maryann, Maryanne, Marylin, Marysa, Masha, Maura, Maure, Maureen, Maurene, Maurine, Maurise, Maurita, Maurizia, Mavra, Meridel, Meriel, Merrili, Mimi, Minette, Minie, Minny, Miriam, Mitzi, Moira, Mollie, Molly, Muire, Murial, Muriel, Murielle
MAUREEN—*O.F.*—dark-skinned; *var.* of Mary.
Maura, Maurene, Maurine, Maurise, Maurita, Maurizia, Moira, Mora, Moreen, Morena, Moria
MAUVE—*Fr.*—plant of the purple mallow.
Maeve, Malva
MEARA—*Gael.*—mirth.
MEGAN—*Gr.*—great; *Gael.*—lovely as a flower; *var.* of Margaret.
Maegan, Maegen, Meaghan, Meg, Megen, Meggi,

Meggie, Meggy, Meghan, Meghann
MELANIE—*Gr.*—dark-skinned.
*Malanie, Mel, Mela, Melania, Melany, Mella,
Melli, Mellie, Melloney, Melly, Mellonie, Melony*
MELANTHA—*Gr.*—dark flower.
MELINDA—*Gr.*—dark, gentle; *Lat.*—honey.
*Linda, Lindy, Linnie, Lynda, Malina, Malinda,
Malinde, Malynda, Mandy, Melinde*
MELISSA—*Gr.*—cherished one filled with
creativity and kindness; honey bee.
*Lissa, Malissa, Mallissa, Mel, Melesa, Melessa,
Melicent, Melisa, Melisande, Melise, Melisenda,
Melisent, Melisse, Melit, Melitta, Mellicent, Mellie,
Mellisa, Melly, Melosa, Milicent, Milissent, Milli,
Millicent, Millie, Millisent, Milly, Misha, Missie,
Missy*
MELODY—*Gr.*—song.
Melodie
MERCEDES—*Sp.*—mercies.
MEREDITH—*Wel.*—guardian from the sea.
Meredithe, Meridith, Merridie, Merry
MERLE—*Lat./Fr.*—blackbird.
*Merl, Merla, Merlina, Merline, Merola, Meryl,
Myrle, Myrlene*
MICHELLE—*Heb.*—who is like the Lord?
inspired by faith, full of goodness and
truth.
*Mechelle, Mia, Micaela, Michaela, Michal, Michel,
Michele, Michelina, Micheline, Michell, Micki,
Mickie, Micky, Midge, Miguela, Miguelita*
MILDRED—*O.E.*—counselor.
MILLICENT—*O.G.*—industrious high power.
*Lissa, Mel, Melicent, Melisande, Melisenda,
Mellicent, Mellie, Mellisent, Melly, Milicent,
Milissent, Milli, Millie, Millisent, Milly*
MIRA—*Lat.*—wonderful; admirable.
*Mireille, Mirella, Mirelle, Mirielle, Mirilla, Myra,
Myrilla*
MIRIAM—*Heb.*—bitter.
Mimi, Mitzi
MOIRA—*Gael.*—great; *var.* of Mary.
Moyra
MONA—*Gr.*—solitary; *Gael.*—noble.
Moina, Monah, Moyna
MONICA—*Lat.*—advisor.
Mona, Monika, Monique
MORGANA—*Wel.*—edge of the sea; bright.
Morgan, Morganica, Morganne, Morgen

MORIAH—*Heb.*—God is my teacher.
MURIEL—*Ar.*—myrrh; *Gael.*—sea-bright.
Meriel, Murial, Murielle
MYRA—*O.F.*—quiet song; *Lat.*—scented oil.
NADINE—*Fr./Sl.*—hope.
*Nada, Nadean, Nadeen, Nadia, Nadiya, Nady,
Nadya, Natka*
NANCY, NAN—graceful; generosity of
spirit, gracious and kind.
*Nana, Nance, Nancee, Nancey, Nanci, Nancie,
Nancy, Nanette, Nanice, Nanine, Nannie, Nanny,
Nanon, Netti, Nettie, Netty*
NAOMI—*Heb.*—pleasant.
Naoma, Noami, Noemi, Nomi
NATALIE—*Lat.*—Christmas, born on
Christmas day.
*Nat, Nata, Natala, Natalee, Natalina, Nataline,
Natalya, Natasha, Nathalia, Nathalie, Natividad,
Natty, Netti, Nettie, Netty*
NEALA—*Celt.*—like a chief; champion.
Neila, Neile, Neilla, Neille
NEDA—*Sl.*—born on Sunday; *O.E.*—wealthy
defender.
Nedda, Nedi
NERISSA—*Gr.*—of the sea.
Nerita
NEVA—*Sp.*—snowy.
Nevada
NICOLE—*Gr.*—victory of the people.
*Colette, Cosetta, Cosette, Nichol, Nichole, Nicholle,
Nicki, Nickie, Nicky, Nichol, Nicola, Nicolea,
Nicolette, Nicoli, Nicolina, Nicoline, Nicolle, Niki,
Nikki, Nikoletta, Nikolia*
NINA—*Sp.*—girl.
Niña, Ninetta, Ninette, Ninnetta, Ninnette, Ninon
NOEL—*Lat./Fr.*—Christmas, born on
Christmas day.
Noelle, Noella, Noellyn, Noelyn, Novelia
NOLA—*Lat.*—small bell; *Gael.*—white
shoulders.
Nolana
NORMA—*Lat.*—rule, pattern.
Noreen
NYDIA—*Lat.*—from the nest.
ODELIA—*Heb.*—I will praise God; *O.E.*—
little and wealthy.
*Odele, Odelinda, Odella, Odelle, Odetta, Odette,
Odilia, Odille, Otha, Othelia, Othilia, Ottilie, Uta*

ODESSA—*Gr.*–long voyage.

OLETHEA—*Lat.*–truth.
Alethea, Oleta

OLGA—*Scan.*–holy.
Elga, Helga, Olenka, Olia, Olive, Olivia, Olva

OLIVIA—*Lat.*–olive tree.
Liv, Liva, Livia, Livvie, Livvy, Nola, Nolana, Nollie, Olga, Olia, Olive, Olivvette, Ollie, Olly, Olva

OLYMPIA—*Gr.*–heavenly.
Olimpia, Olynpe, Olympie

ONEIDA—*N.A.*–expected.
Onida

OPAL—*Hin.*–precious stone.
Opalina, Opaline

OPHELIA—*Gr.*–serpent; help.
Filia, Ofelia, Ofilia, Ophélie, Phelia

ORIANA—*Lat.*–dawning; golden.
Oriane

ORIOLE—*Lat.*–fair-haired.
Auriel, Oriel

PAGE—*Fr.*–useful assistant.
Padge, Paige, Payge

PALOMA—*Sp.*–dove.

PAM—*Gr.*–sweet song of harmony and joy; *var.* of Pamela.

PAMELA—*Gr.*–all-honey.
Pam, Pamelina, Pamelia, Pammi, Pammie, Pammy

PANDORA—*Gr.*–all-gifted.

PATRICIA—*Lat.*–of the nobility; enchanting spirit, full of grace and honor.
Pat, Patrica, Patrice, Patrizia, Patsy, Patti, Patty, Tricia, Trish

PAULA—*Lat.*–small.
Paola, Paolina, Paule, Pauletta, Paulette, Pauli, Paulie, Paulina, Pauline, Paulita, Pauly, Pavla, Polly

PAZIA—*Heb.*–golden.
Paz, Paza, Pazice, Pazit

PEARL—*Lat.*–pearl.
Pearla, Pearle, Pearline, Perl, Perla, Perle, Perry

PEGGY—*Gael.*–filled with sweetness and love; *var.* of Margaret.

PELAGIA—*Gr.*–the sea.
Pelage

PENELOPE—*Gr.*–weaver.
Pen, Penelopa, Penina, Penny

PEPITA—*Sp.*–she shall add.
Pepi, Peta

PERRY—*Fr.*–pear tree; *var.* of Pearl; *Wel.*–son of Harry.
Perrey, Perri

PETRA—*Gr./Lat.*–rock or like a rock.
Perrine, Pet, Peta, Petrina, Petronella, Petrona, Petronilla, Petronille, Pier, Pierette, Pierrette, Pietra

PETULA—*Lat.*–seeker.
Petulah

PETUNIA—*N.A.*–petunia flower.

PHEDRA—*Gr.*–bright.
Faydra, Phaedra, Phaidra

PHILIPPA—*Gr.*–lover of horses.
Felipa, Filippa, Phil, Philipa, Philippe, Philippine, Phillie, Philly, Pippa, Pippy

PHOEBE—*Gr.*–shining; bright.
Phebe

PHYLLIS—*Gr.*–green or leafy bough.
Filide, Philis, Phillis, Phylis, Phyllida, Phyllys

PIA—*It.*–devout; *Lat.*–pious.

PILAR—*Sp.*–pillar.
Pilár

POMONA—*Lat.*–fertile; apple.

PORTIA—*Lat.*–offering.

PRISCILLA—*Lat.*–from ancient times.
Pris, Prisca, Priscella

QUERIDA—*Sp.*–beloved.

QUINN—*O.E.*–queen.

QUINTA—*Lat.*–five; fifth child.
Quentin, Quinn, Quintana, Quintilla, Quintina

QUINTESSA—*Lat.*–essence.
Quintie, Tess, Tessa, Tessie

RACHEL—*Heb.*–ewe; radiant spirit filled with love.
Rachael, Rachele, Rachelle, Rae, Rahel, Rakel, Raquel, Raquela, Ray, Raychel, Rayshell, Rey, Rochell, Shell, Shelley, Shellie, Shelly

RAE—*O.E.*–doe; *Heb.*–var. of Rachel.
Racann, Ralina, Rayna

RAINA—*O.G.*–wise guardian.
Rainah, Raine, Raya, Raylene, Rayna, Raynelle

RAMONA—*Sp.*–mighty or wise protectress.
Ramonda, Ramonia, Romona, Romonda

RAPHAELA—*Heb.*–blessed healer.
Rafa, Rafaela, Rafaelia

REBECCA—*Heb.*–bound; joined; blessing to all, beautiful and elegant.
Becca, Becka, Becki, Beckie, Becky, Bekki, Reba, Rebeca, Rebecka, Rebeka, Rebekah, Rebekkah, Ree, Reeba, Rheba, Riva, Rivalee, Rivi, Rivkah, Rivy

REGINA—*Lat.*—queen.
Raina, Regan, Reggi, Reggie, Regine, Reina, Reine, Reyna, Rina
REIKO—*Jap.*—gratitude, propriety.
RENATA—*Lat.*—reborn.
Renae, Renate, Rene, Renée, Renie, Rennie
RHEA—*Gr.*—earth; that which flows from the earth.
Rea
RHIANNON—*Wel.*—a witch.
Rhiamon, Rhianna, Rianon, Riannon
RHODA—*Gr.*—roses; from Rhodes.
Rhodie, Rhody, Roda, Rodi, Rodie, Rodina
RHONDA—*Wel.*—grand; from the Rhonddra valley.
Ronda
RISA—*Lat.*—laughter.
RIVA—*Fr.*—shore.
Ree, Reeva, Revalee, Rivi, Rivy
ROBERTA—*O.E.*—shining with fame.
Bobbe, Bobbette, Bobbi, Bobbie, Bobby, Bobbye, Bobina, Bobine, Bobinnette, Robbi, Robbie, Robby, Robena, Robenia, Robin, Robina, Robinett, Robinette, Robinia, Ruperta
ROBIN—*O.E.*—robin; var. of Robert.
Robbi, Robbie, Robby, Robbyn, Robena, Robenia, Robina, Robinet, Robinett, Robinette, Robinia, Robyn
ROCHELLE—*Fr.*—from the little rock.
Roch, Rochell, Rochella, Rochette, Roshelle, Shell, Shelley, Shelly
RODERICA—*O.G.*—famous ruler.
Rica
ROLANDA—*O.G.*—fame of the land.
RONA—*Scan.*—mighty power; rough island.
Rhona, Ronalda
ROSALIND—*Sp.*—beautiful rose.
Ros, Rosalinda, Rosalinde, Rosaline, Rosalyn, Rosalynd, Roselin, Roseline, Roslyn, Roz, Rozalin
ROSAMOND—*O.G.*—famous guardian.
Ros, Rosamund, Rosmunda, Rosemonde, Roz, Rozamond
ROSE—*Gr.*—rose.
Rasia, Rhoda, Rhodia, Rhody, Rois, Rosa, Rosaleen, Rosalia, Rosalie, Rosella, Roselle, Rosene, Rosetta, Rosette, Rosie, Rosina, Rosita, Rosy, Rozalie, Roze, Rozele, Rozella, Rozina, Zita
ROSEMARY—*Lat.*—dew of the sea; rosemary.
Rosemaria, Rosemarie
ROWENA—*O.E.*—well-known friend;

Wel.—slender, fair.
Ranna, Rena, Ronni, Ronnie, Ronny, Row, Rowe
ROXANNE—*Pers.*—dawn.
Rosana, Roxane, Roxanna, Roxi, Roxie, Roxine, Roxy
RUBY—*O.F.*—ruby.
Rubetta, Rubi, Rubia, Rubina
RUTH—*Heb.*—friend.
Ruthe, Ruthetta, Ruthi, Ruthina
SABINA—*Lat.*—Sabine woman; woman from Sheba.
Brina, Sabine, Savina
SABRA—*Heb.*—thorny cactus; to rest.
SABRINA—*Lat.*—from the boundary line.
Brina, Sabreena, Zabrina
SACHI—*Jap.*—bliss child; joy.
Sachiko
SALENA—*Lat.*—salty; *Gr.*—moon goddess.
Salina
SALOME—*Heb.*—peace.
Saloma, Salomé, Salomi
SAMANTHA—*Aram.*—listener; told by God.
Sam, Samentha, Sammy
SANDRA—*Gr.*—high-spirited one, guardian and friend; var. of Alexandra.
Sandy
SAPPHIRE—*Gr.*—Sapphire stone; sapphire blue.
Sapphira, Sephira
SARA—*Heb.*—princess.
Sadella, Sadie, Sadye, Saidee, Sal, Salaidh, Sallee, Salli, Sallie, Sally, Sarah, Sarena, Sarene, Sarette, Sari, Sarine, Sarita, Sayre, Shara, Sharai, Shari, Sharon, Sharona, Sher, Sheree, Sheri, Sherie, Sherri, Sherrie, Sherry, Sherye, Sorcha, Sydel, Sydelle, Zara, Zarah, Zaria
SCARLETT
SELENA—*Gr.*—moon; moon goddess.
Celene, Celie, Celina, Celinda, Celine, Sela, Selene, Selia, Selie, Selina, Selinda, Seline, Sena
SELMA—*Scan.*—divinely protected; godly helmet.
Anselma, Zelma
SERAPHINA—*Heb.*—burning, ardent.
Serafina, Serafine, Seraphine
SERENA—*Lat.*—calm, serene.
Reena, Rena, Sarina, Serene
SHANDY—*O.E.*—rambunctious.
SHANLEY—*Gael.*—child of the old hero.
Shanleigh, Shanly

SHANNON—*Gael.*—old; wise.
Channa, Shana, Shandy, Shane, Shani, Shanon, Shanna, Shannah, Shannen, Shauna, Shawna
SHARON—*Heb.*—a plain; vision of beauty, grace, and love.
Charin, Cherin, Shara, Sharai, Shari, Sharla, Sharona, Sherri, Sherrie, Sherry, Sherye
SHEILA—*Gael.*—var. of Cecilia
SHELBY—*O.E.*—from the ledge estate.
SHELLEY—*O.E.*—from the meadow on the ledge.
Shell, Shelli, Shellie, Shelly
SHINA—*Jap.*—good; virtue.
Sheena
SHIRLEY—*O.E.*—from the bright meadow.
Sher, Sheree, Sheri, Sherill, Sherline, Sherri, Sherrie, Sherry, Sherye, Sheryl, Shir, Shirl, Shirlee, Shirleen, Shirlene, Shirline
SHOSHANA—*Heb.*—rose; lily.
SIBLEY—*O.E.*—sibling; having one parent in common.
Sybley
SIBYL—*Gr.*—prophetess; oracle.
Cybil, Cybill, Sib, Sibbie, Sibby, Sibeal, Sibel, Sibella, Sibelle, Sibilla, Sibley, Sibylla, Sibylle, Sybil, Sybila, Sybilla, Sybille
SIGOURNEY—*Fr.*—daring.
SIMONE—*Heb.*—one who hears; listener.
SINEAD—*Ir.*—var. of Jane.
SOPHIE—*Gr.*—wisdom.
Sofia, Sofie, Sonia, Sonja, Sonni, Sonnie, Sonny, Sonya, Sophey, Sophia, Sophronia, Sunny
STEPHANIE—*Gr.*—crowned; charming, considerate, and wise.
Stafani, Stefa, Stefanie, Steffane, Steffi, Steffie, Stepha, Stephana, Stephani, Stephannie, Stephenie, Stephi, Stephie, Stephine, Stesha, Stevana, Stevena
SUE—*Heb.*—delicate one of grace and beauty; var. of Susan.
SUSAN—*Heb.*—lily; graceful one, delicate and beautiful.
Siusan, Sosanna, Sue, Sukey, Suki, Susana, Susanetta, Susann, Susanna, Susannah, Susanne, Susette, Susi, Suie, Susy, Suzanna, Suzanne, Suzette, Suzi, Suzie, Suzy, Suzzy, Zsa Zsa
SYDNEY—*O.F.*—from the city of St. Denis.
Sydel, Sydelle
SYLVIA—*Lat.*—from the forest.
Silva, Silvana, Silvia, Silvie, Zilvia
TABITHA—*Aram.*—gazelle.

Tabatha, Tabbi, Tabbie, Tabbitha, Tabby
TALIA—*Gr.*—blooming; heaven's dew.
Tallia, Tallie, Tally, Talyah, Thalia
TAMARA—*Heb.*—palm tree.
Tamar, Tamarah, Tamarra, Tamera, Tamina, Tammi, Tammie, Tammy, Tamra
TAMMY—*Heb.*—prefection; gentle voice, strong spirit.
Tammi, Tammie
TANSY—*Gr.*—immortality; *Lat.*—tenacious; persistent.
Tandi, Tandie, Tandy, Tanzy
TARA—*Gael.*—rocky pinnacle.
Tarah, Tarra, Tarrah, Terra
TATE—*O.E.*—to be cheerful.
Tatum
TAYLOR—*M.E.*—a tailor.
Tayler
TESSA—*Gr.*—fourth, fourth child; var. of Theresa.
Tess, Tessi, Tessie, Tessy
THALIA—*Gr.*—joyful; blooming.
THEA—*Gr.*—goddess.
THEODORA—*Gr.*—gift of God.
Dora, Fedora, Feodora, Ted, Tedda, Teddi, Teddie, Teddy, Tedi, Tedra, Teodora, Theadora, Theda, Thekla, Theo, Theodosia
THERESA—*Gr.*—reaper; harvest.
Tera, Teresa, Terese, Teresina, Teresita, Teressa, Teri, Terri, Terrie, Terry, Terrye, Terza, Tess, Tessa, Tessi, Tessie, Tessy, Thérèse, Tracey, Tracie, Tracy, Tresa, Tressa, Trescha, Zita
THORA—*Scan.*—thunder; Thor's struggle.
Thordia, Thordis, Tyra
TIA—*Gr.*—princess; *Sp.*—aunt.
TOBY—*Heb.*—God is good.
Tobe, Tobey, Tobi, Tobye, Tova, Tove, Tybi, Tybie
TRACY—*Gael.*—battler; *Lat.*—courageous; var. of Theresa.
Tracee, Tracey, Traci, Tracie
TRILBY—*O.E.*—a soft hat.
Trilbi, Trilbie
TRISTA—*Lat.*—melancholy, sad.
Tris
TRUDY—*O.G.*—beloved; strong spear.
Truda, Trude, Trudey, Trudi, Trudie
TWYLA—*M.E.*—woven of double thread.
Twila
UDELE—*O.E.*—prosperous.
Udelle

ULA—*Celt.*—sea gem.
Eula, Ulla

UMEKO—*Jap.*—plum-blossom child.

UNA—*Lat.*—one, united.
Ona, Oona

URSULA—*Lat.*—little bear.
Orsa, Orsola, Sula, Ulla, Ursa, Ursala, Ursola, Ursulina, Ursuline

VALENTINA—*Lat.*—strong; healthy.
Teena, Teina, Tina, Val, Vale, Valeda, Valene, Valencia, Valentia, Valentine, Valera, Valida, Valina, Valli, Vallie, Vally

VALERIE—*Lat.*—strong.
Val, Valaree, Valaria, Vale, Valeria, Valérie, Valery, Valerye, Valli, Vallie, Vally, Valry

VANESSA—*Gr.*—butterfly.
Nessa, Nessi, Nessie, Nessy, Van, Vania, Vanna, Vanni, Vannie, Vanny

VANORA—*Wel.*—white wave.

VERA—*Lat.*—true; *Sl.*—faith.
Veradis, Vere, Verena, Verene, Verina, Verine, Verla

VERDA—*Lat.*—young, fresh.
Verdi, Verdie

VERENA—*O.G.*—defender; *Lat.*—truth.

VERONICA—*Lat./Gr.*—true image.
Rana, Ronica, Ronna, Ronni, Ronnica, Ronnie, Ronny, Vera, Veronika, Veronike, Véronique, Vonni, Vonnie, Vonny

VICTORIA—*Lat.*—victory.
Vicci, Vicki, Vickie, Vicky, Vikki, Vikky, Viktorine, Vitoria, Vittoria

VIOLET—*Lat.*—violet flower; purple.
Eolande, Iolande, Iolanthe, Jolanda, Vi, Viola, Violante, Viole, Violetta, Violette, Yolanda, Yolande, Yolane, Yolanthe

VIRGINIA—*Lat.*—virginal, maidenly.
Ginelle, Ginger, Ginni, Ginnie, Ginny, Jinny, Virgie, Virginie

VIVIAN—*Lat.*—full of life.
Vevay, Vi, Viv, Vivi, Vivia, Viviana, Vivianne, Vivie, Vivien, Vivienne, Vivyan, Vivyanne

WALLIS—*O.E.*—from Wales.
Wallie, Wally, Wallys

WANDA—*O.G.*—wanderer.
Vanda, Wandie, Wandis, Wenda, Wendeline, Wendi, Wendie, Wendy, Wendye

WHITNEY—*O.E.*—from the white island; from fair water.

WILHELMINA—*O.G.*—determined guardian.
Billi, Billie, Billy, Guglielma, Guillema, Guillemette, Min, Mina, Minna, Minni, Minnie, Minny, Valma, Velma, Vilhelmina, Vilma, Wileen, Wilhelmine, Willa, Willabella, Willamina, Willetta, Willette, Willi, Willie, Willy, Wilma, Wilmette, Wylma

WINIFRED—*O.G.*—peaceful friend; *Wel.*—holy peacemaker.
Freddi, Freddie, Freddy, Fredi, Ona, Oona, Una, Winnifred, Winnie, Winne, Winny, Wynn

WINONA—*N.A.*—first-born daughter.
Wenona, Wenonah, Winnie, Winny, Winonah

WREN—*O.E.*—wren.

WYNNE—*Wel.*—fair, pure.
Winne, Winnie, Winny, Wynn

XANTHE—*Gr.*—golden yellow.
Xantha, Zanthe

XAVIERA—*Ar.*—brilliant; *Sp.*—owner of the new house.

XENIA—*Gr.*—hospitable, welcoming.
Xena, Zena, Zenia

XYLIA—*Gr.*—of the wood.
Xylina

YASU—*Jap.*—the tranquil.

YETTA—*O.E.*—to give; *var.* of Henrietta.

YOKO—*Jap.*—the positive.

YOLANDA—*Gr.*—violet flower.
Eolande, Iolande, Iolanthe, Jolantha, Yolanda, Yolane, Yolanthe

YOSHIKO—*Jap.*—good.
Yoshi

YVONNE—*O.F.*—archer.
Evonne, Ivonne, Yevette, Yvette

ZARA—*Heb.*—dawn.
Zarah, Zaria

ZELDA—*O.G.*—gray warrior; *var.* of Griselda.

ZENOBIA—*Gr.*—sign, symbol; power of Zeus.
Cenobia, Zeba, Zeeba, Zeena, Zena

ZETTA—*Heb.*—olive.
Zeta, Zetana

ZIA—*Lat.*—grain.
Zea

ZINA—*Af.*—name.

ZOE—*Gr.*—life.
Zoë

ZOLA—*It.*—lump of earth.

ZORA—*Sl.*—light of dawn.
Zorah, Zorana, Zorina, Zorine

AARON—*Heb.*—enlightened; exalted.
Aharon, Aranne, Ari, Arin, Arnie, Arny, Aron, Arron, Erin, Haroun

ABRAHAM—*Heb.*—father of the multitude.
Abe, Abey, Abie, Abram, Abran, Avram, Avrom, Bram, Ibrahim

ADAIR—*Gael.*—from the oak tree ford.

ADAM—*Heb.*—man of the red earth.
Ad, Adamo, Adams, Adan, Addie, Addy, Ade, Adhamh

ADRIAN—*Lat.*—from Adria.
Ade, Adriano, Adrien, Hadrian

AIDAN—*Gael.*—fire; warmth of the home.
Aiden

ALAN—*Gael.*—handsome; cheerful; peaceful.
Ailin, Al, Alain, Alair, Aland, Alann, Alano, Alanson, Alanus, Allan, Allayne, Allen, Alley, Alleyn, Allie, Allyn, Alon

ALASTAIR—*Gael.*—form of Alexander.
Al, Alasdair, Alasteir, Alaster, Alistair, Alister, Allister

ALBERT—*O.E.*—highborn; noble and bright.
Adelbert, Ailbert, Al, Alberto, Albie, Albrecht, Aubert, Bert, Bertie, Berty, Elbert

ALDEN—*O.E.*—old friend.
Al, Aldin, Aldwin, Elden, Eldin

ALEXANDER—*Gr.*—helper, defender of mankind.
Alec, Alejandro, Alejo, Alek, Aleksandr, Allesandro, Alex, Alexandr, Alexandre, Alexandro, Alexandros, Alexio, Alexis, Alic, Alick

ALFRED—*O.E.*—elf counselor; wise counselor.
Al, Alf, Alfie, Alfredo, Alfy, Avery

ALI—*Ar.*—exalted; greatest.
Aly

ALPHONSE—*O.G.*—noble and eager; eager for battle.
Al, Alf, Alfie, Alfons, Alfonso, Alfonzo, Alford, Alfy, Alonso, Alonzo, Alphonso, Fons, Fonsie, Fonz, Fonzie, Lon, Lonnie

ALTON—*O.E.*—old town.

ALVIN—*O.G.*—old or noble friend.
Al, Aloin, Aluin, Aluino, Alva, Alvan, Alvie, Alvy, Alvyn, Alwin, Alwyn, Elvin, Elwin

AMIEL—*Heb.*—lord of my people.

AMOS—*Heb.*—borne by God.

ANATOLE—*Gr.*—from the east.
Anatol, Anatolio

ANDREW—*Gr.*—strong; manly.
Anders, Andie, Andonis, Andre, Andrea, Andreas, Andrej, Andres, Andrés, Andrey, Andrius, Andy

ANGELO—*Gr.*—messenger; angel.

ANGUS—*Gael.*—unique choice; one strength.
Ennis, Gus

ANSEL—*O.F.*—follower of a nobleman.
Ancell, Ansell

ANSON—*O.G.*—son of divine origin.
Annson, Hanson

ANTHONY—*Lat.*—invaluable; priceless.
Antin, Antoine, Anton, Antone, Antoni, Antonin, Antonino, Antonio, Antonius, Antons, Antony

ARCHIBALD—*O.G.*—valorous; bold.
Arch, Archaimbaud, Archambault, Archer, Archibaldo, Archibold, Archie, Archy

ARDEN—*Lat.*—ardent, fiery, enthusiastic.

ARIEL—*Heb.*—lion of God.

ARISTOTLE—*Gr.*—superior; best.

ARLEN—*Gael.*—pledge.
Arlan, Arles, Arlin

ARMAND—*O.G.*—army man.
Arman, Armando, Armin

ARNOLD—*O.G.*—strong as an eagle; eagle-ruler.
Arnaldo, Arnaud, Arne, Arney, Arni, Arnie, Arnoldo, Arny

ARTHUR—*Celt.*—bear; stone.
Art, Artair, Arte, Arther, Arthor, Artie, Artur, Arturo, Artus, Arty

ARVIN—*O.E.*—friend of the people; friend of the army.

ASA—*Heb.* physician.

ASHER—*Heb.*—happy.

ASHFORD—*O.E.*—ash-tree ford.

ASHLEY—*O.E.*—ash tree meadow.
Ash, Asheley, Ashlan, Ashlin

AUBREY—*O.F.*—elf ruler.
Alberik, Aube, Auberon, Avery, Oberon

AVERILL—*M.E.*—April; boar-warrior.
Ave, Averell, Averil

AXEL—*O.G.*—father of peace.
Aksel, Ax, Axe, Axil

BAILEY—*O.F.*—bailiff.
Baile, Bailie, Baillie, Baily

BAIRD—*Gael.*—balladeer; singer.
Bar, Bard, Barde, Barr

BALDWIN—*O.G.*—bold friend.
Bald, Balduin, Baudoin

BARCLAY—*O.E.*—birch tree meadow.
Bar, Bark, Barklay, Berkeley, Berkie, Berkley, Berky

BARNABAS—*Gr.*—son of comfort or

consolation.
Barnaba, Barnabe, Barnaby, Barnebas, Barney, Barnie, Barny, Burnaby, Nab

BARNETT—*O.E.*—nobleman.
Barn, Barney, Baronett, Barron

BARRET—*O.G.*—strong as a bear.
Bar, Barratt, Barrett, Bear

BARTON—*O.E.*—from the barley farm.
Barrton, Bart, Bartie, Barty

BARUCH—*Heb.*—blessed.

BASIL—*Lat.*—kingly.
Base, Basile, Basilio, Basilius, Vasilis, Vassily

BAXTER—*O.E.*—baker.

BEAUMONT—*Fr.*—beautiful hill.

BEAUREGARD—*O.F.*—beautiful face or expression.
Beau, Bo

BELLAMY—*O.F.*—handsome friend.
Belamy, Bell

BENEDICT—*Lat.*—blessed.
Ben, Bendick, Bendict, Bendix, Benedetto, Benedick, Benedicto, Benedikt, Bengt, Benito, Bennie, Bennt, Benny, Benoit, Bent

BENJAMIN—*Heb.*—son of the right hand.
Ben, Beniamino, Benjamen, Benji, Benjie, Benjy, Benn, Bennie, Benny, Benyamin, Jamie, Jim

BENTON—*O.E.*—moor or coarse grass.

BERNARD—*O.G.*—brave bear.
Barnard, Barney, Barnie, Barny, Bear, Bearnard, Bern, Bernardo, Bernarr, Berne, Bernhard, Bernhardo, Bernie, Berny, Burnard

BERTRAM—*O.E.*—glorious raven.
Bart, Bartram, Beltran, Bert, Bertie, Berton, Bertrand, Bertrando, Berty

BEVAN—*Gael.*—son of Evan.
Bev, Beven, Bevin, Bevon

BJORN—*Scan.*—bear.

BLAINE—*Gael.*—thin, slender.
Blane, Blayne

BLAIR—*Gael.*—plain; flat land.

BLAKE—*O.E.*—pale and fair.

BOGART—*O.F.*—strong as a bow.

BOONE—*O.F.*—good.

BOOTH—*O.E.*—dwelling place; hut.
Boot, Boote, Boothe

BORDEN—*O.E.*—valley of the boar.

BORG—*Scan.*—castle.

BORIS—*Slav.*—battler, warrior.

BOWIE—*Gael.*—blond.

Bow, Bowen, Boyd

BOYCE—*O.F.*—woodland.

BRADEN—*O.E.*—wide valley.

Bradan, Brade, Bradin

BRADFORD—*O.E.*—broad river crossing.

BRADLEY—*O.E.*—wide meadow.

Brad, Bradly, Bradney, Lee, Leigh

BRADSHAW—*O.E.*—large forest.

BRADY—*O.E.*—broad island.

BRAMWELL—*O.E.*—of Abraham's well; where the broom sage grows.

BRANDON—*O.E.*—beacon hill.

Bran, Brand, Branden, Brandy, Brandyn, Brannon

BRENDAN—*Gael.*—stinky hair.

Bren, Brenden, Brendin, Brendis, Brendon, Brennan, Brennen, Bryn

BRENTON—*O.E.*—from the steep hill.

Brent, Brentyn

BRETT—*Celt.*—Briton.

Bret, Bretton, Brit, Britt

BREWSTER—*O.E.*—brewer.

BRIAN—*Gael.*—strength.

Briano, Briant, Brien, Brion, Bryan, Bryant, Bryen, Bryon

BRIGHAM—*O.E.*—enclosed bridge; village near the bridge.

BROCK—*O.E.*—badger.

BRODERICK—*O.E.*—brother; broad ridge.

Brod, Broddie, Broddy, Broderic

BRODY—*Gael.*—ditch.

Brodee, Brodie

BRONSON—*O.E.*—the brown man's son.

Bron, Bronnie, Bronnson, Bronny

BROOK—*O.E.*—stream; brook.

Brooke, Brookes, Brooks

BRUCE—*O.F.*—brushwood thicket.

BRUNO—*It.*—brown-haired or dark-skinned.

BURGESS—*O.E.*—citizen, especially of a fortified town.

Burg, Burgiss, Burr

BURKE—*O.F.*—fortified settlement.

Berk, Berke, Bourke, Burk

BURNE—*O.E.*—brook; stream.

Bourn, Bourne, Burn, Byrne

BURRIS—*O.E.*—of the town.

BURTON—*O.E.*—fortress.

CAESAR—*Lat.*—hairy; emperor.

Casar, Cesar, Cesare, Cesaro, Kaiser, Seasar

CALDWELL—*O.E.*—cold spring.

CALEB—*Heb.*—bold one; dog.

Cal, Cale, Kaleb

CALHOUN—*Celt.*—narrow woods; warrior.

CALVERT—*O.E.*—herdsman.

Cal, Calbert

CALVIN—*Lat.*—bald.

Cal, Calv, Kalvin, Vin, Vennie, Vinny

CAMDEN—*Gael.*—winding valley.

CAMERON—*Gael.*—crooked nose.

Cam, Carney, Cammy

CAMPBELL—*Gael.*—crooked mouth.

CANUTE—*Scan.*—knot.

Cnut, Knut, Knute

CARLETON—*O.E.*—farmer's village.

Carl, Carlton, Charlton

CARLISLE—*O.E.*—fortified town or tower.

Carl, Carlie, Carly, Carlyle

CARMINE—*Lat.*—song.

CARNEY—*Gael.*—victorious; winner.

Car, Carny, Karney, Kearney

CARSON—*O.E.*—son of the marsh dwellers.

CARTER—*O.E.*—cart driver or maker.

CARVER—*O.E.*—woodcarver.

CASEY—*Gael.*—brave.

CASPER—*Pers.*—treasurer or treasure guard.

Caspar, Cass, Cassie, Cassy, Gaspar, Gaspard, Gasparo, Gasper, Jasper, Kaspar, Kasper

CASSIDY—*Gael.*—clever.

Cass, Cassady, Cassie, Cassy

CASSIUS—*Lat.*—vain.

CECIL—*Lat.*—blind.

Cece, Cecile, Cecilio, Cecilius, Celio

CEDRIC—*O.E.*—war chieftain.

Cad, Caddaric, Ced, Rick, Richie, Ricky

CHADWICK—*O.E.*—soldier's town.

CHAIM—*Heb.*—life.

Haim, Hayim, Hy, Hyman, Hymie, Mannie, Manny

179

CHALMERS—*Gael.*—son of the lord.

CHANDLER—*O.F.*—candlemaker.
Chan, Chane.

CHANEY—*Fr.*—oak tree.
Cheney

CHANNING—*O.E.*—knowing.

CHAPMAN—*O.E.*—merchant; peddler.

CHARLES—*O.G.*—man; strong.
Carl, Carlo, Carlos, Carrol, Carroll, Cary, Caryl, Chad, Chaddie, Chaddy, Charley, Charlie, Charlot, Charlton, Chas

CHAUNCEY—*M.E.*—chancellor.
Chan, Chance, Chancey, Chaunce

CHESTER—*O.E.*—fortified camp or town.

CHRISTIAN—*Gr.*—follower of Christ.
Chretien, Chris, Chrissie, Chrissy, Christiano, Christie, Christy, Cristian, Kit, Kris, Krispin, Kristian

CHRISTOPHER—*Gr.*—Christ-bearer.
Christoffer, Christoforo, Christoper, Christoph, Christophe, Christophorus, Cris, Cristobal, Cristoforo, Christos, Kit, Kristo, Kristofer, Kristofor, Kristoforo, Kristos

CLARENCE—*Lat.*—bright; famous.
Clair, Clarance, Clare

CLARK—*O.F.*—scholar.
Clarke, Clerc, Clerk

CLAUDE—*Lat.*—lame.
Claudell, Claudian, Claudianus, Claudio, Claudius, Claus

CLAYBORNE—*O.E.*—born of the earth.
Claiborn, Claiborne, Clay, Clayborn, Claybourne

CLAYTON—*O.E.*—farm built on clay.

CLEMENT—*Lat.*—merciful.
Clem, Clemens, Clemente, Clementius, Clemmie, Clemmy, Clim, Klemens, Klement, Kliment

CLEVELAND—*O.E.*—cliff or high area.
Cleavland, Cleve, Clevy, Clevie

CLIFFORD—*O.E.*—cliff at the river crossing.

CLIFTON—*O.E.*—town near the cliffs.

CLINTON—*O.E.*—headland farm.

CLYDE—*Gael.*—rocky eminence; heard from afar; *Wel.*—warm.

CODY—*O.E.*—a cushion or pillow.

COLBERT—*O.E.*—outstanding seafarer.
Cole, Colt, Colvert, Culbert

COLBY—*O.E.*—dark farm.
Cole

COLEMAN—*O.E.*—adherent of Nicholas.
Cole, Colman

COLIN—*Gael.*—child; youth.
Cailean, Colan, Cole, Collin

COLLIER—*O.E.*—miner.
Colier, Colis, Collayer, Collis, Collyer, Colyer

COLTON—*O.E.*—dark village; coal town.

CONLAN—*Gael.*—hero.
Con, Conlen, Conley, Conlin, Conn

CONNOR—*Gael.*—high desire.

CONRAD—*O.G.*—honest or brave counselor.
Conrade, Conrado, Cort, Koenraad, Konrad, Kort, Kurt

CONWAY—*Gael.*—holy river.

COOPER—*O.E.*—barrelmaker.

CORBETT—*Lat.*—raven.
Corbet, Corbie, Corbin, Corby

CORDELL—*O.F.*—ropemaker.
Cord, Cordie, Cordy, Cory

CORNELIUS—*Lat.*—like a horn.
Conney, Connie, Conny, Cornall, Cornell, Corney, Cornie, Corny, Cory, Neel, Nelly

COSMO—*Gr.*—order, harmony, the universe.
Cos, Cosimo, Cosme, Cozmo

COURTLAND—*O.E.*—from the farmstead or court land.

COURTNEY—*O.F.*—court member.
Cort, Court, Courtnay, Curt

COWAN—*Gael.*—hillside hollow.
Coe, Cowey, Cowie

CRAIG—*Gael.*—crag; rock.

CRANDALL—*O.E.*—the cranes' valley.
Cran, Crandal, Crandell

CRAWFORD—*O.E.*—ford of the crows.

CREIGHTON—*O.E.*—rocky place.
Creigh, Creight, Crichton

CRISPIN—*Lat.*—curly haired.

CROSBY—*Scan.*—from or at the shrine of the cross.
Crosbie, Cross

CULLEN—*Gael.*—handsome.
Cull, Cullan, Culley, Cullie, Cullin, Cully

CURRAN—*Gael.*—hero.

CURTIS—*O.F.*—courteous.
Curcio, Curt, Curtice, Kurtis

CYRIL—*Gr.*—lordly.
Cirillo, Cirilo, Cy, Cyrill, Cyrille, Cyrillus

CYRUS—*Pers.*—sun.

DALE—*O.E.*—valley.
Dael, Dal, Dayle

DALLAS—*Gael.*—wise; skilled.
Dal, Dall, Dallis

DALTON—*O.E.*—the village or estate in the valley.

DAMIAN—*Gr.*—to tame.
Dame, Damiano, Damien, Damon

DANA—*Scan.*—from Denmark.
Dane

DANIEL—*Heb.*—God is my judge.
Dan, Dani, Dannial, Danill, Dannel, Dannie, Danny

DANTE—*Lat.*—lasting; enduring.

DARBY—*Gael.*—free man; *O.N.*—from the deer estate.
Dar, Darb, Darbee, Derby

DARCY—*Gael.*—dark; *O.F.*—from Arcy.
D'Arcy, Dar, Darce

DARIUS—*Gr.*—wealthy.

DARNELL—*O.E.*—hidden place.
Dar, Darn, Darnall

DARREL—*Fr.*—beloved; darling.
Dare, Darral, Darrell, Darrill, Darryl, Daryl, Daryle, Derril

DARREN—*Gael.*—great.
Dare, Daren, Darin, Daron, Darrin, Darron, Derron

DARWIN—*O.E.*—dear friend.
Derwin, Derwynn

DAVID—*Heb.*—beloved.
Dav, Dave, Davey, Davidde, Davide, Davidson, Davie, Davin, Davis, Daven, Davon, Davy, Dov

DAVIS—*O.E.*—son of David.

DEAN—*O.E.*—valley.
Deane, Dene, Deyn, Dino

DELANEY—*Gael.*—child of the challenger.
Delainey, Delany

DELBERT—*O.E.*—bright as day.
Bert, Bertie, Berty, Dalbert, Del

DEMETRIUS—*Gr.*—following Demeter.
Demetre, Demetri, Demetris, Dimitri, Dimitry, Dmitri

DEMPSEY—*Gael.*—proud.

DENNIS—*Gr.*—of Dionysus.
Den, Denis, Dennet, Denney, Dennie, Dennison, Denny, Denys, Dion, Dionisio, Dionysus, Ennis

DENVER—*O.E.*—green valley.

DEREK—*O.G.*—rule of the people.
Darrick, Deric, Derick, Derrek, Derrick, Derrik, Derk, Dirk

DERRY—*Gael.*—red-haired; from Derry.

DESMOND—*Gael.*—man from south Munster.
Des, Desi, Desmund

DEVIN—*Gael.*—poet.
Dev, Devon, Devy

DEVLIN—*Gael.*—brave; fierce.
Dev, Devland, Devlen

DEWEY—*Wel.*—prized; var. of David.

DOMINIC—*Lat.*—belonging to the Lord.
Don, Domenic, Domenico, Domingo, Dominick, Dominik, Dominique, Nick, Nickie, Nicky

DONALD—*Gael.*—world ruler; world power.
Don, Donal, Donall, Donalt, Donaugh, Donn, Donnell, Donnie, Donny

DONNELLY—*Gael.*—brave, brown-haired man.
Don, Donn, Donnell, Donnie, Donny

DONOVAN—*Gael.*—dark warrior.
Don, Donavon, Donn, Donnie, Donny

DOUGLAS—*Gael.*—black water.
Doug, Dougie, Douglass, Dougy, Dugaid

DOVEV—*Heb.*—to whisper.
Dov

DOYLE—*Gael.*—dark stranger.

DRAKE—*M.E.*—owner of the Sign of the Dragon inn.

DREW—*O.F.*—sturdy; *Wel.*—wise.
Dru, Drud, Drugi

DUANE—*Gael.*—little and dark; swarthy.
Dewain, Dwain, Dwayne

DUNCAN—*Gael.*—dark-skinned fighter.

DUNHAM—*Celt.*—dark man.

DUSTIN—*O.G.*—brave fighter.

Dust, Dustan, Dustie, Duston
DYLAN—*Wel.*—from the sea.
Dilan, Dill, Dillie, Dilly
EARL—*O.E.*—nobleman.
Earle, Earlie, Early, Erl, Erle, Errol, Erroll, Erryl, Rollo
EDGAR—*O.E.*—rich spearman.
Ed, Eddie, Eddy, Edgard, Edgardo
EDMUND—*O.E.*—rich protector.
Eadmund, Eamon, Ed, Edd, Eddie, Edmon, Edmond, Edmondo, Ned
EDWARD—*O.E.*—happy or wealthy protector.
Ed, Eddie, Eddy, Edik, Edouard, Eduard, Eduardo, Edvard, Ewart
EDWIN—*O.E.*—rich friend.
Eadwinn, Ed, Eddie, Eddy, Edlin, Eduino, Lalo, Ned, Neddie, Neddy
ELIJAH—*Heb.*—Jehovah is God.
El, Eli, Elia, Elias, Elihu, Aliot, Elliott, Ellis, Ely, Elyott
ELLERY—*O.E.*—elder tree island.
Ellary, Ellerey
ELLSWORTH—*O.E.*—nobleman's estate.
Ellswerth, Elsworth
ELTON—*O.E.*—old town.
Alden, Aldon, Eldon
ELVIS—*Scan.*—all wise.
Al, Alvis, Alvys, El
ELWOOD—*O.E.*—from the old wood.
EMERSON—*O.G.*—son of the industrious ruler.
EMERY—*O.G.*—industrious ruler.
Amerigo, Amery, Amory, Emmerich, Emmerie, Emmery, Emory
EMIL—*Lat.*—flattering, winning.
Emelen, Emile, Emilio, Emlen, Emlyn
EMMANUEL—*Heb.*—God is with us.
Eman, Emanuel, Emanuele, Immanuel, Mannie, Manny, Manuel.
ENGELBERT—*O.G.*—bright as an angel.
Bert, Bertie, Berty, Englebert, Ingelbert, Inglebert
EPHRAIM—*Heb.*—fruitful; productive.
Efren, Efren, Ephrem
ERIC—*Scan.*—all ruler; ever-powerful.
Erek, Erich, Erick, Erik, Errick, Eryk, Rick, Rickie, Ricky

ERNEST—*O.E.*—earnest; sincere.
Ernesto, Ernestus, Ernie, Ernst, Erny
ETHAN—*Heb.*—firm.
EUGENE—*Gr.*—well-born.
Eugen, Eugene, Eugenio, Eugenius, Gene
EVAN—*Wel.*—young warrior; *var.* of John.
Ev, Even, Evin, Evyn, Ewan, Ewen, Owen
FABIAN—*Lat.*—bean grower.
Fabe, Fabek, Faber, Fabert, Fabiano, Fabien, Fabio
FALKNER—*O.E.*—falconer.
Faulkner, Fowler
FARRELL—*Gael.*—hero.
Farr, Farrel, Ferrel, Ferrell
FELIX—*Lat.*—fortunate.
Fee, Felic, Felice, Felicio, Felike, Feliks, Felizio
FELTON—*O.E.*—village or camp on the meadow.
FENTON—*O.E.*—marshland farm.
FERDINAND—*O.G.*—daring voyager.
Ferd, Ferdie, Ferdo, Ferdy, Fergus, Fernando, Hernando
FERGUS—*Gael.*—supreme choice.
Fearghas, Fergie, Ferguson
FERRIS—*Gael.*—var. of Peter, the rock.
Farris, Ferriss
FIDEL—*Lat.*—faithful.
Fidele, Fidelio
FINLAY—*Gael.*—little fair-haired soldier.
Fin, Findlay, Findley, Finley, Finn
FITZGERALD—*O.E.*—son of the spear ruler.
Fitz, Gerald, Gerrie, Gerry, Jerry
FITZPATRICK—*O.E.*—son of a nobleman.
FLEMING—*O.E.*—a Dutchman.
Flem, Flimming
FLETCHER—*M.E.*—arrow-featherer, fletcher.
Flecher, Fletch
FLYNN—*Gael.*—son of the red-haired man.
FORBES—*Gael.*—field.
FOREST, FORREST—*O.F.*—forest; woodsman.
Forester, Forrester, Forster, Foss, Foster
FOWLER—*O.E.*—trapper of wild fowl.
FRANCIS—*Lat.*—a Frenchman.
Chico, Fran, Francesco, Franchot, Francisco, Franciskus, Francois, Frank, Frankie, Franky, Frannie, Franny, Frans, Fransisco, Frants

FRANKLIN—*M.E.*—free landowner.
Fran, Francklin, Francklyn, Frank, Frankie, Franklyn, Franky

FRAZER—*O.E.*—curly-haired.
Fraser, Frasier, Fraze, Frazier

FREDERICK—*O.G.*—peaceful ruler.
Eric, Erich, Erick, Erik, Federico, Fred, Freddie, Freddy, Fredek, Frederic, Frederich, Frederico, Frederigo, Frederik, Fredric, Fredrick, Friedrich, Friedrick

FREEMAN—*O.E.*—free man.
Free, Freedman, Freeland, Freemon

FREMONT—*O.G.*—guardian of freedom.

FULBRIGHT—*O.G.*—very bright.
Fulbert, Philbert

FULLER—*O.E.*—one who shrinks cloth.

FULTON—*O.E.*—a field near the town.

GABRIEL—*Heb.*—hero of God.
Gabbie, Gabby, Gabe, Gabi, Gabie, Gabriele, Gabriello, Gaby, Gavriel

GALEN—*Gael.*—healer; calm.
Gaelan, Gale, Gayle

GANNON—*Gael.*—fair-skinned.

GARDNER—*M.E.*—gardener.
Gar, Gard, Gardener, Gardie, Gardiner, Gardy

GARETH—*Wel.*—gentle.
Gar, Garth

GARFIELD—*O.E.*—spear field.

GARLAND—*O.E.*—from the battlefield;
O.F.—wreath.

GARNER—*O.F.*—armed sentry; grain gatherer.

GARRICK—*O.E.*—spear-rule.
Garek, Garik, Garrek, Garrik

GARVEY—*Gael.*—rough peace.

GARY—*O.E.*—spear.
Gare, Garey, Garry

GAVIN—*Wel.*—white hawk.
Gav, Gavan, Gaven, Gawain, Gawen

GEORGE—*Gr.*—farmer.
Egor, Georas, Geordie, Georg, Georges, Georgie, Georgy, Giorgio, Goran, Jorgan, Jorge, Yurik

GERALD—*O.G.*—spearruler.
Egor, Garald, Garold, Gary, Gearalt, Gearard, Gerard, Gerek, Gerick, Gerik, Gerrard, Gerri, Gerrie, Gerry, Giraldo, Giraud, Jerald, Jerrie, Jerrold, Jerry, Jorgen, Jurek, Yurik, Ygor

GIDEON—*Heb.*—feller of trees; destroyer.

GILBERT—*O.E.*—trusted; bright pledge.
Gilberto, Gilburt, Gill, Giselbert, Guilbert, Wilbert, Wilbur, Wilburt, Will

GILROY—*Gael.*—devoted to the red-haired man.
Gil, Gildray, Gill, Gillie, Gilly, Roy

GLENDON—*Gael.*—village in the valley.
Glen, Glenden, Glenn

GODDARD—*O.G.*—divinely firm.
Godard, Godart, Goddart, Godhart, Gothart, Gotthardt

GORDON—*O.E.*—hill on the meadows or plains.
Gordan, Gorden, Gordie, Gordy

GRADY—*Gael.*—noble, illustrious.
Gradiegh, Gradey

GRAHAM—*O.E.*—the gray home.
Graehme, Graeme, Gram

GRANGER—*O.E.*—farmer.

GRANT—*Fr.*—tall; great.
Grantham, Granthem, Grantley, Grenville

GRANTLAND—*O.E.*—great plains.

GREGORY—*Lat.*—watchman; watchful.
Graig, Greg, Gregg, Greggory, Gregoire, Gregoor, Gregor, Gregorio, Gregorious

GRIFFITH—*Wel.*—fierce chief; ruddy.

GROVER—*O.E.*—from the grove.

GUTHRIE—*Gael.*—from the windy place;
O.G.—war hero.
Guthrey, Guthry

GUY—*Fr.*—guide; *O.G.*—warrior.
Guido

HADLEY—*O.E.*—from the heath.
Had, Hadlee, Hadleigh, Lee, Leigh

HALDAN—*Scan.*—half-Danish.
Hal, Halden, Halfdan, Halvdan

HALEY—*Gael.*—ingenious; hay meadow.
Hailey, Haily, Hal, Hale, Haliegh, Lee, Leigh

HALSEY—*O.E.*—from Hal's island.

HAMID—*Ar.*—thanking God.

HAMILTON—*O.E.*—proud or beloved estate.

HANLEY—*O.E.*—high meadow.
Hanlea, Hanleigh, Henleigh, Henley

HARDY—*O.G.*—bold; brave, daring.

183

HARLAN—*O.E.*–from the army land.
Harland, Harlen, Harlin

HARLEY—*O.E.*–from the long field.
Arley

HARLOW—*O.E.*–from the rough hill or army-hill.
Arlo

HAROLD—*Scan.*–army-ruler.
Araldo, Hal, Harald, Haroldas, Harry, Herold, Herrick

HARPER—*O.E.*–harp player.

HARTLEY—*O.E.*–deer meadow.

HARVEY—*O.G.*–strong and ardent.
Harv, Herve, Hervey

HASIN—*In.*–laughing.
Hasen, Hassin

HASKEL—*Heb.*–understanding and intellect.
Haskell

HASTINGS—*O.E.*–son of the stern man.

HAVELOCK—*Scan.*–sea battle.

HAYDEN—*O.E.*–from the hedged valley.
Haydon

HAYES—*O.E.*–from the hedged place.

HEATH—*M.E.*–from the heath.

HENRY—*O.G.*–ruler of an estate.
Arrigo, Enrico, Enrique, Hal, Hank, Harry, Heike, Heindrick, Heinrich, Heinrik, Hendrick, Hendrik, Henri, Henrik

HILARY—*Lat.*–cheerful.
Hi, Hilaire, Hilario, Hilarius, Hill, Hillary, Hillery, Hillie, Hilly, Ilario

HILLEL—*Heb.*–greatly praised.

HILTON—*O.E.*–town on the hill.

HOGAN—*Gael.*–youth.

HOLBROOK—*O.E.*–brook near the hollow.
Brook, Holbrooke

HOLDEN—*O.E.*–the hollow in the valley.

HOLLIS—*O.E.*–grove of holly trees.

HOLMES—*M.E.*–from the river islands.

HOLT—*O.E.*–woods; forest.

HORTON—*O.E.*–from the gray estate.
Hort, Horten, Orton

HOUSTON—*O.E.*–hill town.

HOWARD—*O.E.*–watchman.

HUGH—*O.E.*–intelligence.

HUMPHREY—*O.G.*–peaceful Hun.
Hum, Humfrey, Humfrid, Humfried, Hump, Humph, Hunfredo, Onfre, Onfroi, Onofredo

HUNTER—*O.E.*–hunter.

HUNTINGTON—*O.E.*–hunting estate.
Hunt, Huntingdon

HUNTLEY—*O.E.*–hunter's meadow.
Hunt, Huntlee, Lee, Leigh

HUSSEIN—*Ar.*–little and handsome.
Husain, Husein

HUTTON—*O.E.*–the house on the bluff.

HUXLEY—*O.E.*–Hugh's meadow.

IAN—*Gael.*–var. of John.
Iain

INGEMAR—*Scan.*–famous son; Ing's son.
Ingamar, Ingmar

INGRAM—*O.E.*–angel; raven.
Inglis, Ingram, Ingrim

INNIS—*Gael.*–island.
Innes, Inness

IRA—*Heb.*–watchful.

IRVING—*Gael.*–beautiful; *O.E.*–sea friend.
Earvin, Erv, Ervin, Erwin, Irv, Irvin, Irvine, Irwin, Irwinn

ISAAC—*Heb.*–he laughs; laughter.
Ike, Ikey, Isaak, Isac, Isacco, Isak, Itzak, Izaak, Izak

ISIDORE—*Gr.*–gift of Isis.
Dore, Dory, Isador, Isadore, Isidor, Isidoro, Isidro, Izzy

ISRAEL—*Heb.*–ruling with the Lord; wrestling with the Lord.

IVAN—*Rus.*–var. of John.

IVAR—*Scan.*–archer.
Ive, Iver, Ivor, Yvon, Yvor

JACOB—*Heb.*–supplanter.
Giacobo, Giacomo, Giacopo, Hamish, Iago, Jack, Jackie, Jacky, Jacobo, Jacques, Jaime, Jake, Jakie

JAMAL—*Ar.*–beauty; handsome.
Jamaal, Jammal

JAMES—*Eng.*–var. of Jacob.
Diego, Giacomo, Giamo, Hamish, Iago, Jacques, Jaime, Jameson, Jamesy, Jamey, Jamie, Jamison, Jay, Jayme, Jim, Jimmie, Jimmy, Seamus, Seumas, Shamus

JARED—*Heb.*–to descend.
Jarad, Jarid, Jarrad, Jarred, Jarrett, Jarrid, Jarrod, Jerad

JARVIS—*O.G.*—keen with a spear.

JASON—*Gr.*—healer.

Jaisen, Jase, Jasen, Jasun, Jay, Jayson

JEDIDIAH—*Heb.*—beloved of the Lord.

JEFFERSON—*O.E.*—son of Jeffrey.

JEFFREY—*O.F.*—heavenly peace.

Geoff, Geoffrey, Godfrey, Gottfried, Jeff, Jefferey, Jeffie, Jeffy, Jeffry

JEREMIAH—*Heb.*—Jehovah exalts.

Dermot, Diarmid, Geremia, Jere, Jereme, Jeremias, Jeremy, Jerry

JEROME—*Lat.*—holy name.

Gerome, Gerrie, Gerry, Hieronymus, Jere, Jereme, Jerrome, Jerry

JESSE—*Heb.*—God exists.

Jess, Jessee, Jessey, Jessie

JESUS—*Heb.*—God will help; God will save.

Chucho, Jecho

JOACHIM—*Heb.*—the Lord will judge.

Akim, Joaquin

JOEL—*Heb.*—Jehovah is the Lord.

JOHN—*Heb.*—God is gracious.

Evan, Ewan, Ewen, Gian, Giavani, Giovanni, Hana, Hans, Iain, Ian, Jack, Jackie, Jacky, Jan, Janos, Jean, Jens, Jock, Jocko, Johan, Johann, Johannes, Johnnie, Johnny, Johny, Jon, Jone, Juan, Owen, Sean, Shaughn, Shaun, Shawn, Zane

JONATHAN—*Heb.*—Jehovah gave; God's gift.

Jonathan, Johnathon, Jon, Jonathon, Yanaton

JORDAN—*Heb.*—descend.

Giordano, Jared, Jerad, Jordon, Jory, Jourdain

JOSEPH—*Heb.*—God shall add or increase.

Che, Giuseppe, Iosep, Jo, Joe, Joey, Jose, Jozef

JOSHUA—*Heb.*—Jehovah saves.

Josh, Joshia, Joshuah

JUDE—*Lat.*—right in the law; praise.

JULIAN—*Lat.*—belonging or related to Julius.

Julien

JULIUS—*Gr.*—youthful.

Giulio, Jolyon, Jule, Jules, Julie, Julio

JUSTIN—*Lat.*—upright; fair.

Giustino, Guisto, Justen, Gustinian, Justino, Justis, Justus

KAREEM—*Ar.*—noble, generous.

Karim

KEANE—*O.E.*—sharp, keen.

Kean, Keen, Keene

KEEFE—*Gael.*—cherished; handsome.

KEEGAN—*Gael.*—small and fiery.

KEENAN—*Gael.*—small and ancient.

KEIR—*Celt.*—dark-skinned.

Kerr

KEITH—*Wel.*—from the forest; *Gael.*—from the battle place.

KELLY—*Gael.*—warrior.

Kele, Kellen, Kelley

KELSEY—*Scan.*—from the ship island.

KELTON—*O.E.*—keel town; town where ships are built.

Keldon, Kelson

KELVIN—*O.E.*—lover of ships.

Kelwin

KENDALL—*O.E.*—from the bright valley; from the valley of the Kent river.

Ken, Kendal, Kendell, Kenn, Kennie, Kenny

KENDRICK—*Gael.*—son of Henry; *O.E.*—royal ruler.

KENLEY—*O.E.*—from the king's meadow.

Kenleigh

KENNEDY—*Gael.*—helmeted chief.

Canaday, Ken, Kenn, Kennie, Kenny

KENNETH—*Gael.*—handsome.

Kennet, Kennith

KENYON—*Gael.*—white-haired; blond.

KERRY—*Gael.*—dark; dark-haired.

Keary

KERWIN—*O.E.*—friend of the marshlands.

KEVIN—*Gael.*—gentle, lovable, handsome.

Kev, Kevan, Keven, Kevon

KIERAN—*Gael.*—small and dark-skinned.

Kiernan

KILLIAN—*Gael.*—small and warlike.

Kilian, Killie, Killy

KIMBALL—*O.E.*—warrior chief; bold ruler.

Kim, Kimbell, Kimble

KINCAID—*Celt.*—battle chief.

KINGSLEY—*O.E.*—from the king's meadow.

King, Kingsly, Kinsley

KINGSTON—*O.E.*—from the king's estate.

KIRBY—*Scan.*—church village.

Kerby

KIRK—*Scan.*–church.
Kerk

KNOX—*O.E.*–from the hills.

KWASI—*Af.*–born on Sunday.

KYLE—*Gael.*–handsome; from the strait.
Kiel, Kile, Kiley, Ky, Kylie

LAMAR—*O.G.*–famous throughout the land; famous as the land.
Lemar

LAMBERT—*O.G.*–bright land; bright as the land.
Bert, Bertie, Berty, Lamberto, Landbert

LAMONT—*Scan.*–lawyer.
Lammond, Lamond, Monty

LANCE—*O.G.*–servant.
Lancelot, Launce

LANE—*M.E.*–narrow road.
Laney, Lanie

LANGDON—*O.E.*–from the long hill.
Landon, Langsdon, Langston

LANGLEY—*O.E.*–from the long meadow.

LATHAM—*Scan.*–from the barn.

LAWFORD—*O.E.*–a ford on the hill.

LAWRENCE—*Lat.*–from Laurentium; laurel-crowned.
Larry, Lars, Lauren, Laurence, Laurens, Laurent, Laurie, Lauritz, Lawry, Lenci, Lon, Lonnie, Lonny, Lornat, Loren, Lorens, Lorenzo

LAWTON—*O.E.*–from the town on the hill.
Laughton, Law

LEIF—*Scan.*–beloved.

LEIGHTON—*O.E.*–from the meadow village.
Lay, Layton

LELAND—*O.E.*–meadow land.
Lee, Lealand, Leeland, Leigh

LEONARD—*O.G.*–bold lion.
Lee, Len, Lenard, Lennard, Lennie, Lenny, Leo, Leon, Leonardo, Leonerd, Leonhard, Leonid, Leonidas, Lonnard, Lonnie, Lonny

LEROY—*O.F.*–king.
Elroy, Lee, Leigh, Leroi, LeRoy, Roy

LESLIE—*Gael.*–from the gray castle.
Lee, Leigh, Les, Lesley, Lezlie

LESTER—*Lat.*–from the chosen camp;

O.E.–from Leicester.
Leicester, Les

LEVI—*Heb.*–joined.
Levey, Levin, Levon, Levy

LINCOLN—*O.E.*–from the town by the pool.

LINDSAY—*O.E.*–linden tree island.
Lind, Lindsey

LIONEL—*O.F.*–lion cub.

LIVINGSTON—*O.E.*–Leif's town.

LLEWELLYN—*Wel.*–lionlike; lightning.
Lew, Lewis, Llywellyn

LLOYD—*Wel.*–gray-haired.
Floyd, Loy, Loydie

LOGAN—*Gael.*–from the small hollow.

LOUIS—*O.G.*–renowned warrior.
Aloysius, Lew, Lewis, Lou, Louie, Lucho, Ludvig, Ludwig, Luigi, Luis

LOWELL—*O.F.*–little wolf.
Lovell, Loew

LUCIAN—*Lat.*–shining, light.
Luciano, Lucien

LUCIUS—*Lat.*–bringer of light; *Gr.*–from Lucanus.
Luca, Lucais, Lucas, Luce, Lucias, Lucio, Lukas, Luke

LUTHER—*O.G.*–famous warrior.
Lothaire, Lothario, Lutero

LYLE—*O.F.*–from the island.
Lisle, Ly, Lyell

LYNDON—*O.E.*–from the linden tree hill.
Lin, Lindon, Lindy, Lyn, Lynn

MACKENZIE—*Gael.*–son of the wise leader.

MADISON—*O.E.*–son of the powerful warrior.

MALCOLM—*Gael.*–follower of St. Columba.

MALIK—*Mus.*–master.

MALLORY—*O.G.*–army counselor; *O.F.*–unhappy.

MARCEL—*Lat.*–little and warlike.
Marcello, Marcellus, Marcelo

MARK—*Lat.*–warlike.
Marc, Marcos, Marcus, Mario, Marius, Markos, Markus

MARLON—*O.F.*–little falcon.

Marlin
MARLOW—*O.E.*–the hill by the lake.
Mar, Marlo, Marlowe
MARSHALL—*O.F.*–steward; horse-keeper.
MARTIN—*Lat.*–warlike.
Mart, Martainn, Marten, Martie, Martijn, Martino, Marty, Martyn
MARVIN—*O.E.*–lover of the sea.
Marv, Marve, Marven, Marwin, Mervin, Merwin, Merwyn, Murvyn
MASON—*O.F.*–stoneworker.
MATTHEW—*Heb.*–gift of the Lord.
Mata, Mateo, Mathe, Mathew, Mathian, Mathias, Matias, Matt, Matteo, Matthaeus, Matthaus, Mattheus, Matthias, Matthieu, Matthiew, Mattias, Mattie, Matty
MAURICE—*Lat.*–dark-skinned.
Mauricio, Maurie, Maurise, Marits, Maurizio, Maury, Morey, Morie, Moritz, Morris
MAXWELL—*O.E.*–large well; the important man's well.
MAYNARD—*O.G.*–powerful, strong.
May, Mayne, Menard
MELBOURNE—*O.E.*–mill stream.
Mel, Melborn, Melburn
MELVILLE—*O.E./O.F.*–town of the hard worker.
MELVIN—*Gael.*–polished chief.
Mal, Malvin, Mel, Melvyn, Vin, Vinnie, Vinny
MEREDITH—*Wel.*–guardian from the sea; great ruler.
Merideth, Merry
MERLIN—*M.E.*–falcon.
Marlin, Marlon, Merle
MERRILL—*O.E.*–famous.
Merill, Merle, Merrel, Merrell, Meryl
MERTON—*O.E.*–from the town by the sea.
Merv, Merwyn, Murton
MEYER—*Ger.*–farmer; *Heb.*–bringer of light.
Meier, Meir, Myer
MICHAEL—*Heb.*–who is like the Lord?
Micah, Michail, Michal, Michale, Micheal, Micheil, Michel, Michele, Mickey, Mickie, Micky, Miguel, Mikael, Mike, Mikel, Mikey, Mikkel, Mikol, Mishca, Mitch, Mitchel, Mitchell, Mychal

MILES—*Lat.*–soldier; *O.G.*–merciful.
Milo, Myles
MILTON—*O.E.*–from the mill town.
MONROE—*Gael.*–mouth of the Roe River.
Monro, Munro, Munroe
MONTAGUE—*Fr.*–from the pointed mountain.
MONTGOMERY—*O.E.*–from the rich man's mountain.
Monte, Monty
MORGAN—*Gael.*–bright; white; from the edge of the sea.
Morgen, Morgun
MORTON—*O.E.*–town near the moor.
Morten
MUHAMMAD—*Ar.*–praised.
Hamid, Hammad, Mahmoud, Mahmud, Mohammed
MURDOCK—*Gael.*–sailor.
Murdoch
MURRAY—*Gael.*–sailor.
Morey, Murry
MYRON—*Gr.*–fragrant ointment.
NAPOLEON—*Gr.*–lion of the woodland dell; *It.*–from Naples.
NATHANIEL—*Heb.*–gift of God.
Nat, Nataniel, Nate, Nathan, Nathanael, Nathanial, Natty
NEIL—*Gael.*–champion.
Neal, Neale, Neall, Nealon, Neel, Neill, Neils, Nels, Nial, Niall, Niel, Niels, Nil, Niles, Nils
NEVILLE—*O.F.*–new town.
Nev, Nevil, Nevile
NEVIN—*Gael.*–worshipper of the saint; *O.E.*–nephew.
Nefen, Nev, Nevins, Niven
NEWTON—*O.E.*–new town.
NICHOLAS—*Gr.*–victory of the people.
Klaus, Niccolo, Nichole, Nichols, Nick, Nickey, Nickie, Nickolas, Nickolaus, Nicky, Nicol, Nicolai
NIGEL—*Gael.*–champion.
NOAH—*Heb.*–wandering; rest.
NOBLE—*Lat.*–well-born.
NOEL—*Fr.*–the Nativity; born at Christmas.

Natal, Natale, Nowell

NOLAN—*Gael.*—famous; noble.

Noland

NORMAN—*O.F.*—Norseman; northerner.

Norm, Normand, Normie, Normy

NORRIS—*O.F.*—man from the north; nurse.

NORTHROP—*O.E.*—northern farm.

North, Northrup

NORTON—*O.E.*—northern town.

OAKLEY—*O.E.*—from the oak-tree field.

Oak, Oakes, Oakie, Oakleigh, Oaks

ODELL—*Scan.*—little and wealthy.

OGDEN—*O.E.*—oak valley or hill.

Ogdan, Ogdon

OLIVER—*Lat.*—olive tree; *Scan.*—kind, affectionate.

Noll, Nollie, Nolly, Olivero, Olivier, Oliviero, Ollie, Olly, Olvan

OMAR—*Ar.*—first son; highest; follower of the Prophet.

OREN—*Heb.*—pine tree; *Gael.*—pale-skinned.

Oran, Orin, Oren, Orrin

ORLAND/ORLANDO—*O.E.*—from the famous land.

Land, Lannie, Lanny, Orlan

ORSON—*Lat.*—bearlike.

OSBORN—*O.E.*—warrior of God; *Scan.*—divine bear.

Osborne, Osbourn, Osbourne

OSMOND—*O.E.*—divine protector.

Esme, Osmund, Ozzie, Ozzy

OTTO—*O.G.*—rich

Odo, Othello, Otho

PAGE—*Fr.*—youthful assistant.

Padget, Padgett, Paige

PALMER—*O.E.*—palm-bearer.

PARKER—*M.E.*—guardian of the park.

PARRISH—*M.E.*—from the churchyard.

PASCAL—*It.*—pertaining to Easter or Passover; born at Easter or Passover.

Pascale, Pace, Pasquale, Patsy

PATRICK—*Lat.*—nobleman.

Paddey, Paddie, Paddy, Padraic, Padraig, Padriac, Pat, Patton, Patric, Patrice, Patricio, Patrizio

PATTON—*O.E.*—from the warrior's estate

or town.

Pat, Paten, Patin, Paton, Patten

PAUL—*Lat.*—small.

Pablo, Pall, Paolo, Paulie, Pauly, Pavel, Poul

PAXTON—*Lat.*—from the peaceful town.

Packston, Paxon

PERCIVAL—*O.F.*—pierce the valley.

Parsifal, Perceval, Percy, Purcell

PERRY—*M.E.*—pear tree; *O.F.*—little Peter.

PETER—*Gr.*—rock.

Farris, Ferris, Parry, Peadar, Pearce, Peder, Pedro, Peirce, Perkin, Perren, Perry, Pete, Peterus, Petey, Petr, Pierce, Pierre, Pierson, Pieter, Pietrek, Pietro, Piotr

PEYTON—*O.E.*—from the warrior's estate.

Pate, Payton

PHILIP/PHILLIP—*Gr.*—lover of horses.

Felipe, Filip, Filippo, Phil, Philipp, Phillipe, Phillipp, Pippo

PORTER—*Lat.*—gatekeeper.

POWELL—*Celt.*—alert.

PRENTICE—*M.E.*—apprentice.

Pren, Prent, Prentiss

PRESCOTT—*O.E.*—from the priest's cottage.

PRESTON—*O.E.*—from the priest's estate.

PRICE—*Wel.*—son of the ardent one; Rhys' son.

Brice, Bryce, Pryce

PUTNAM—*O.E.*—dweller by the pond.

QUENTIN—*Lat.*—fifth; fifth child.

Quent, Quinn, Quint, Quintin, Quinton, Quintus

QUILLAN—*Gael.*—cub.

QUINCY—*O.F.*—from the fifth son's estate.

QUINLAN—*Gael.*—physically strong.

RADCLIFFE—*O.E.*—red cliff.

RAFFERTY—*Gael.*—rich and prosperous.

Rafe, Raff, Raffarty

RAFI—*Ar.*—exalting.

Raffi, Raffin

RALEIGH—*O.E.*—from the red deer meadow.

Lee, Leigh, Rawley

RALPH—*O.E.*—wolf-counselor.

Rafe, Raff, Ralf, Raoul, Rolf, Rolph

RAMSAY—*O.E.*—from the ram's island;

from the raven's island.

Ram, Ramsey

RANCE—*Af.*—borrowed all.

RANDOLPH—*O.E.*—shield-wolf.

Rand, Randal, Randall, Randell, Randolf, Randy

RANSOM—*O.E.*—son of the shield.

RAPHAEL—*Heb.*—God has healed.

Falito, Rafael, Rafaelle, Rafaello

RAVI—*Hin.*—sun.

Ravid, Raviv

RAYBURN—*O.E.*—from the deer brook.

RAYMOND—*O.E.*—mighty or wise
protector.

*Raimondo, Raimund, Raimundo, Ramon, Ray,
Raymund, Raemonn*

RAYNOR—*Scan.*—mighty army.

Ragnar, Rainer, Ray, Rayner

REDFORD—*O.E.*—from the red river
crossing.

REECE—*Wel.*—enthusiastic; fiery.

Rees, Resse, Rhys, Rice

REED—*O.E.*—red-haired.

Read, Reade, Reid

REGAN—*Gael.*—little king.

Reagan, Reagen, Regen

REGINALD—*O.E.*—powerful and mighty.

*Reg, Reggie, Reggis, Reginauld, Reinald, Reinaldo,
Reinaldos, Reinhold, Herinold, Renwald, Renault,
Rene, Reynold, Reynolds, Rinaldo*

REMINGTON—*O.E.*—from the raven estate.

REUBEN—*Heb.*—behold, a son.

Reuven, Rouvin, Rube, Ruben, Rubin, Ruby

REX—*Lat.*—king.

RICHARD—*O.G.*—powerful ruler.

*Dick, Dickie, Dicky, Ric, Ricard, Ricardo, Riccardo,
Rich, Richardo, Richart, Richie, Richy, Rick,
Rickard, Rickert, Rickey, Ricki, Rickie, Ricky, Rico,
Riki, Riocard*

RICHMOND—*O.G.*—powerful protector.

RIDER—*O.E.*—horseman.

Rydder, Ryder

RILEY—*Gael.*—valiant.

Reilly, Ryley

RIORDAN—*Gael.*—bard, royal poet.

RIPLEY—*O.E.*—from the shouter's meadow.

ROARKE—*Gael.*—famous ruler.

Rorke, Rourke

ROBERT—*O.E.*—bright fame.

*Bob, Bobbie, Bobby, Rab, Riobard, Rip, Rob, Robb,
Robbie, Robby, Robers, Roberto, Robin, Rupert,
Ruperto, Ruprecht*

ROCKWELL—*O.E.*—from the rocky spring.

RODERICK—*O.G.*—famous ruler.

*Roderic, Roderich, Roderigo, Rodrick, Rodrigo,
Rodrique, Rory, Rurik, Ruy*

RODNEY—*O.E.*—island near the clearing.

ROGER—*O.G.*—famous spearman.

*Rodge, Rodger, Rog, Rogerio, Rogers, Rudiger,
Ruggiero, Rutger, Ruttger*

ROLAND—*O.G.*—from the famous land.

*Lannie, Lanny, Rolando, Roldan, Roley, Rolland,
Rollie, Rollin, Rollins, Rollo, Rowland*

RONALD—*O.E.*—powerful counsel.

Ranald, Ron, Ronnie, Ronny

ROONEY—*Gael.*—red-haired.

Rowan, Rowen, Rowney

ROOSEVELT—*O.D.*—from the rose field.

RORY—*Gael.*—red king.

ROSS—*O.F.*—red; *Gael.*—headland.

ROY—*O.F.*—king.

Roi, Ruy

RUDYARD—*O.E.*—from the red enclosure.

RUSSELL—*Fr.*—red-haired; fox-colored.

RUTHERFORD—*O.E.*—from the cattle ford.

RUTLEDGE—*O.E.*—from the red pool.

RYAN—*Gael.*—little king.

Ryon, Ryun

SALVATORE—*It.*—savior.

*Sal, Sallie, Sally, Salvador, Salvidor, Sauveur,
Xaviero, Zaviero*

SAMUEL—*Heb.*—told by or asked of God.

Sam, Sammie, Sammy, Samuele, Shem

SANBORN—*O.E.*—from the sandy brook.

SANDERS—*M.E.*—son of Alexander.

*Sander, Sanderson, Sandor, Sandy, Saunders,
Saunderson*

SANFORD—*O.E.*—sandy river crossing.

SAWYER—*M.E.*—sawer of wood;
woodworker.

SCOTT—*O.E.*—Scotsman.

SEAN—*Ir.*—var. of John.

Shane, Shaughn, Shaun, Shawn

SEBASTIAN—*Lat.*—venerated; majestic.

Bastian, Bastien, Sebastiano, Sebastien

SELBY—*O.E.*–the village by the mansion.

SELDON—*O.E.*–the willow tree valley.
Don, Donnie, Donny, Selden, Shelden

SELWYN—*O.E.*–friend from the palace.

SEYMOUR—*O.F.*–from St. Maur.

SHANNON—*Gael.*–small and wise; ancient.
Shanan, Shannan

SHAW—*O.E.*–from the grove.

SHEA—*Gael.*–from the fairy fort.
Shae, Shay

SHEEHAN—*Gael.*–small and peaceful.

SHELBY—*O.E.*–from the ledge estate.

SHELDON—*O.E.*–the farm or village on the ledge.
Shell, Shelley, Shelly, Shelton

SHERBORN—*O.E.*–from the clear brook.
Sherborne, Sherburn, Sherburne

SHERIDAN—*Gael.*–wild man.

SHERLOCK—*O.E.*–fair-haired.
Sherlocke, Shurlock, Shurlocke

SHERMAN—*O.E.*–shearer.

SIDNEY—*O.F.*–from St. Denis.
Sid, Sidnee, Syd, Sydney

SIMON—*Heb.*–he who hears.
Si, Sim, Simeon, Simmonds, Simone, Syman, Symon

SINCLAIR—*O.F.*–from St. Clair.
Clair, Clare, Sinclare

SLOAN—*Gael.*–warrior.

SOLOMON—*Heb.*–peaceful.

SOMERSET—*O.E.*–summer settlement.

SPENCER—*M.E.*–dispenser of provisions.
Spence, Spense, Spenser

STAFFORD—*O.E.*–riverbank landing place.
Staffard, Staford

STANFORD—*O.E.*–from the rocky ford.
Ford, Stan, Standford, Stanfield

STANLEY—*O.E.*–from the rocky meadow.
Stan, Stanleigh, Stanly

STANTON—*O.E.*–from the stony farm.

STEPHEN—*Gr.*–crown.
Esteban, Estevan, Etienne, Stefan, Stefano, Steffen, Sthepan, Stephanus, Steve, Steven, Stevie

STERLING—*O.E.*–valuable.
Stirling

STUART—*O.E.*–caretaker; steward.
Steward, Stewart, Stu

SVEN—*Scan.*–youth.
Svend, Swen

SYLVESTER—*Lat.*–from the woods.
Silvester, Sly

TALBOT—*O.G./Fr.*–valley-bright.

TANNER—*O.E.*–leather worker, tanner.

TARO—*Jap.*–first born male.

TATE—*M.E.*–cheerful.

TAVISH—*Gael.*–twin.

TAYLOR—*M.E.*–tailor.

TEMPLETON—*O.E.*–village of the temple.

TERENCE—*Lat.*–smooth.
Tarrance, Terencio, Terrance, Terrence, Terry

TERRILL—*O.G.*–belonging to Thor; martial.

THADDEUS—*Gr.*–courageous; *Lat.*–praiser.
Tad, Tadd, Taddeo, Taddeusz, Tadeo, Tadio, Thad, Thaddaus

THATCHER—*O.E.*–roof thatcher.

THAYER—*O.F.*–from the nation's army.

THEODORE—*Gr.*–gift of God.
Feodor, Teador, Ted, Tedd, Teddie, Teddy, Teodoor, Teodor, Teodoro

THOMAS—*Aram./Heb.*–twin.
Thom, Thoma, Tom, Tomas, Tommie, Tommy

THORNTON—*O.E.*–thorny farm or village.

THORPE—*O.E.*–from the village.

THURSTON—*Scan.*–Thor's stone.
Thorstein, Thorsten, Thurstan

TIMOTHY—*Gr.*–honoring God.

TOBIAS—*Heb.*–the Lord is good.
Tobiah, Tobie, Tobin, Tobit, Toby

TODD—*M.E.*–fox.

TRACY—*Gael.*–battler; *Lat.*–courageous.

TRAVIS—*O.F.*–at the crossroads; toll collector.
Traver, Travers, Travus, Travys

TRENT—*Lat.*–torrential waters.
Trenton

TREVOR—*Gael.*–prudent.
Trefor, Trev, Trevar, Trever

TREY—*M.E.*–three, the third.

TRISTAN—*Wel.*–sorrowful.
Tris, Tristan, Tristram

TROY—*Gael.*–foot soldier.

TRUMAN—*O.E.*–faithful man.
Trueman, Trumaine, Trumann

TUCKER—*O.E.*–fuller or tucker of cloth.
TURNER—*Lat.*–one who works the lathe.
TYLER—*O.E.*–maker of tiles.
ULRIC—*O.G.*–wolf-ruler.
Alaric, Ulrich, Ulrick
UPTON—*O.E.*–from the upper town.
URIEL—*Heb.*–God is my flame.
Uri, Yuri
VALENTINE—*Lat.*–strong; healthy.
Val, Valentijn, Valentin, Valentino
VALERIAN—*Lat.*–strong.
Valerien, Valerio, Valery
VANCE—*M.E.*–thresher.
VAUGHN—*Wel.*–small.
VERNON—*Lat.*–springlike, youthful;
O.F.–alder grove.
Lavern, Vern, Verne, Verney
VICTOR—*Lat.*–conqueror.
Vic, Vick, Victoir, Vittorio
VINCENT—*Lat.*–conquering.
Vin, Vince, Vinnie, Vinny
VIRGIL—*Lat.*–rod or staff bearer.
Verge, Vergil, Virge, Virgie
VITO—*Lat.*–alive.
VLADIMIR—*Slav.*–powerful prince.
Vladamir
WADE—*O.E.*–advancer; from the river
crossing.
WAINWRIGHT—*O.E.*–wagonmaker.
WALKER—*O.E.*–thickener of cloth, fuller.
WALLACE—*O.E.*–Welshman.
Wallache, Wallas, Wallie, Wallis, Wally, Walsh, Welch,
Welsh
WALTER—*O.G.*–powerful warrior.
Gauthier, Gualterio, Gualtiero, Wallie, Wally, Walt,
Walther, Wat
WALTON—*O.E.*–from the walled town.
WARD—*O.E.*–guardian; watchman.
WARNER—*O.G.*–armed defender.
Werner, Wernher
WARREN—*O.G.*–defender; watchman.
WASHINGTON—*O.E.*–from the town of
one known for astuteness.
WAYLAND—*O.E.*–from the land by the road.
Waylen, Waylin, Waylon, Weylin

WAYNE—*O.E.*–wagoner.
WESLEY—*O.E.*–western meadow.
Lee, Leigh, Wes, Westleigh, Westley
WESTON—*O.E.*–from the western
settlement.
WHITNEY—*O.E.*–from the white island;
from fair water.
WHITTAKER—*O.E.*–from the white field.
WILEY—*O.E.*–from the water meadow.
Willey, Wylie
WILLARD—*O.G.*–resolutely brave; willful.
WILLIAM—*O.E.*–determined guardian.
Bill, Billie, Billy, Guglielmo, Guillaume, Guillermo,
Liam, Wilek, Wilhelm, Will, Willem, Willi, Willie,
Willis, Willy, Wilmar
WILTON—*O.E.*–from the farm by the
spring.
WINFIELD—*O.E.*–from a friend's field.
WINTHROP—*O.E.*–from the friendly village.
WOODROW—*O.E.*–from the passage in
the woods.
WYATT—*O.F.*–little warrior.
WYNDHAM—*Gael.*–from the village near
the winding road.
XAVIER—*Ar.*–bright.
Javier, Xever
XENOPHON—*Gr.*–strange voice.
XYLON—*Gr.*–from the forest.
YANCY—*N.A.*–Englishman.
YARDLEY—*O.E.*–from the enclosed
meadow.
YASIR—*Ar.*–well to do.
Yaseer, Yasser
YEHUDI—*Heb.*–praise of the Lord.
YORK—*O.E.*–estate of the boar.
YVES—*Fr.*–yew wood.
Ives, Ivo, Yvo
ZACHARY—*Heb.*–Jehovah hath
remembered.
Zachariah, Zacharias, Zacharie, Zechariah, Zeke
ZALMAN—*Heb.*–peaceable.
ZANE—*Eng.*–var. of John.
ZEBULON—*Heb.*–giving honor.
Zeb, Zebulen